PRISM
READING

Student's Book

1

Michele Lewis
Richard O'Neill

with
Christina Cavage

CAMBRIDGE
UNIVERSITY PRESS

CAMBRIDGE
UNIVERSITY PRESS

University Printing House, Cambridge CB2 8BS, United Kingdom

One Liberty Plaza, 20th Floor, New York, NY 10006, USA

477 Williamstown Road, Port Melbourne, VIC 3207, Australia

314–321, 3rd Floor, Plot 3, Splendor Forum, Jasola District Centre, New Delhi – 110025, India

79 Anson Road, #06–04/06, Singapore 079906

Cambridge University Press is part of the University of Cambridge.

It furthers the University's mission by disseminating knowledge in the pursuit of education, learning and research at the highest international levels of excellence.

www.cambridge.org
Information on this title: www.cambridge.org/9781108556194

© Cambridge University Press 2018

First published 2018

20 19 18 17 16 15 14 13 12 11 10 9 8 7 6 5 4 3 2 1

Printed in Malaysia by Vivar Printing

A catalogue record for this publication is available from the British Library

ISBN 978-1-108-55619-4 Prism Reading 1 Student's Book with Online Workbook
ISBN 978-1-108-45530-5 Prism Reading 1 Teacher's Manual

CONTENTS

Scope and Sequence   4

How *Prism Reading* Works   8

What Makes *Prism Reading* Special   12

UNIT 1   Places   14

UNIT 2   Festivals and Celebrations   32

UNIT 3   The Internet and Technology   50

UNIT 4   Weather and Climate   68

UNIT 5   Sports and Competition   86

UNIT 6   Business   104

UNIT 7   People   122

UNIT 8   The Universe   140

Glossary of Key Vocabulary   158

Video Scripts   162

Credits   167

Advisory Panel   168

SCOPE AND SEQUENCE

UNIT	READING PASSAGES	KEY READING SKILLS	ADDITIONAL READING SKILLS	
1 PLACES *Disciplines* Sociology / Urban Planning	1 Rise of the Megacities (report) 2 Homestay Vacations: A Home away from Home (online article)	Scanning for numbers Using a T-chart	Understanding key vocabulary Previewing Reading for main ideas Reading for details Scanning to find information Working out meaning Scanning to predict content Taking notes Making inferences Synthesizing	
2 FESTIVALS AND CELEBRATIONS *Disciplines* Anthropology / Cultural Studies	1 Celebrate! (article) 2 Muscat Festival: A Celebration of Omani Culture (online article)	Previewing	Understanding key vocabulary Using your knowledge Taking notes Reading for details Recognizing text type Scanning to predict content Reading for main ideas Making inferences Synthesizing	
3 THE INTERNET AND TECHNOLOGY *Disciplines* Computer Science / Engineering	1 Tech Expert Today: Someone's Always Watching You Online (online article) 2 Video Games for Kids: Win, Lose, or Draw? (essay)	Reading for main ideas Making inferences	Understanding key vocabulary Scanning to predict content Reading for details Using your knowledge Taking notes Recognizing text type Synthesizing	
4 WEATHER AND CLIMATE *Disciplines* Environmental Studies / Meteorology	1 Extreme Weather (book excerpt) 2 Surviving the Sea of Sand: How to Stay Alive in the Sahara Desert (article)	Reading for details Using your knowledge to predict content	Understanding key vocabulary Reading for main ideas Recognizing text type Synthesizing	

LANGUAGE DEVELOPMENT	WATCH AND LISTEN	SPECIAL FEATURES
Nouns, verbs, and adjectives	The Top U.S. City	Critical Thinking Collaboration
Prepositions of time and place Adverbs of frequency	The Meaning of Independence Day	Critical Thinking Collaboration
Compound nouns Giving opinions	Predictive Advertising	Critical Thinking Collaboration
Collocations with *temperature* Describing a graph	Tornadoes	Critical Thinking Collaboration

UNIT	READING PASSAGES	KEY READING SKILLS	ADDITIONAL READING SKILLS	
5 SPORTS AND COMPETITION _Disciplines_ Sports Management / Sports Science	1 Five Unusual Sports (online article) 2 Tough Guy: A Race to the Limit (article)	Scanning to predict content	Understanding key vocabulary Reading for main ideas Reading for details Recognizing text type Previewing Predicting content using visuals Taking notes Understanding discourse Working out meaning Synthesizing	
6 BUSINESS _Disciplines_ Business / Marketing	1 Are You Ready for the World of Work? (survey) 2 The Story of Google (online article)	Working out meaning from context Annotating	Understanding key vocabulary Scanning to predict content Reading for main ideas Reading for details Giving opinions Identifying audience Making inferences Synthesizing	
7 PEOPLE _Disciplines_ Psychology / Sociology	1 Incredible People: Ben Underwood (blog post) 2 Role Models (blog posts)	Using a Venn diagram	Understanding key vocabulary Scanning to predict content Reading for main ideas Reading for details Taking notes Working out meaning Identifying purpose Previewing Making inferences Synthesizing	
8 THE UNIVERSE _Disciplines_ Astronomy / Engineering	1 The New Space Race: The Rise of Commercial Space Travel (online article) 2 Is There Life on Other Planets? (essay)	Identifying the author's purpose	Understanding key vocabulary Using your knowledge Previewing Reading for main ideas Reading for details Scanning to predict content Annotating Distinguishing fact from opinion Synthesizing	

LANGUAGE DEVELOPMENT	WATCH AND LISTEN	SPECIAL FEATURES
Prepositions of movement	Skiing in the French Alps	Critical Thinking Collaboration
Collocations with *business* Business vocabulary	Amazon's Fulfillment Center	Critical Thinking Collaboration
Noun phrases with *of* Adjectives to describe people	The 101-Year-Old Weather Volunteer	Critical Thinking Collaboration

Giving evidence and supporting
  an argument
Infinitives of purpose
	Going to the International
	  Space Station
		Critical Thinking
		Collaboration

1 READING

Receptive, language, and analytical skills

Students improve their reading skills through a sequence of proven activities. First they study key vocabulary to prepare for each reading and to develop academic reading skills. Then they work on synthesis exercises in the second reading that prepare students for college classrooms. Language Development sections teach vocabulary, collocations, and language structure.

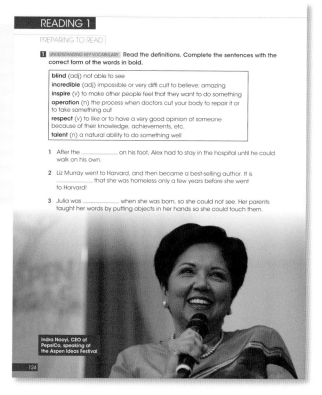

READING 1

PREPARING TO READ

1 UNDERSTANDING KEY VOCABULARY Read the definitions. Complete the sentences with the correct form of the words in bold.

> **blind** (adj) not able to see
> **incredible** (adj) impossible or very difficult to believe; amazing
> **inspire** (v) to make other people feel that they want to do something
> **operation** (n) the process when doctors cut your body to repair it or to take something out
> **respect** (v) to like or to have a very good opinion of someone because of their knowledge, achievements, etc.
> **talent** (n) a natural ability to do something well

1 After the _____ on his foot, Alex had to stay in the hospital until he could walk on his own.

2 Liz Murray went to Harvard, and then became a best-selling author. It is _____ that she was homeless only a few years before she went to Harvard!

3 Julia was _____ when she was born, so she could not see. Her parents taught her words by putting objects in her hands so she could touch them.

Indra Nooyi, CEO of PepsiCo, speaking at the Aspen Ideas Festival

124

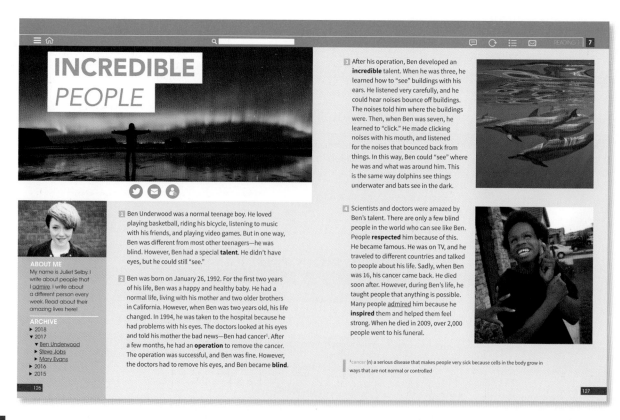

INCREDIBLE
PEOPLE

ABOUT ME
My name is Juliet Selby. I write about people that I <u>admire</u>. I write about a different person every week. Read about their amazing lives here!

ARCHIVE
▶ 2018
▼ 2017
  ▼ Ben Underwood
  ▶ Steve Jobs
  ▶ Mary Evans
▶ 2016
▶ 2015

1 Ben Underwood was a normal teenage boy. He loved playing basketball, riding his bicycle, listening to music with his friends, and playing video games. But in one way, Ben was different from most other teenagers—he was blind. However, Ben had a special **talent**. He didn't have eyes, but he could still "see."

2 Ben was born on January 26, 1992. For the first two years of his life, Ben was a happy and healthy baby. He had a normal life, living with his mother and two older brothers in California. However, when Ben was two years old, his life changed. In 1994, he was taken to the hospital because he had problems with his eyes. The doctors looked at his eyes and told his mother the bad news—Ben had cancer[1]. After a few months, he had an **operation** to remove the cancer. The operation was successful, and Ben was fine. However, the doctors had to remove his eyes, and Ben became **blind**.

3 After his operation, Ben developed an **incredible** talent. When he was three, he learned how to "see" buildings with his ears. He listened very carefully, and he could hear noises bounce off buildings. The noises told him where the buildings were. Then, when Ben was seven, he learned to "click." He made clicking noises with his mouth, and listened for the noises that bounced back from things. In this way, Ben could "see" where he was and what was around him. This is the same way dolphins see things underwater and bats see in the dark.

4 Scientists and doctors were amazed by Ben's talent. There are only a few blind people in the world who can see like Ben. People **respected** him because of this. He became famous. He was on TV, and he traveled to different countries and talked to people about his life. Sadly, when Ben was 16, his cancer came back. He died soon after. However, during Ben's life, he taught people that anything is possible. Many people <u>admired</u> him because he **inspired** them and helped them feel strong. When he died in 2009, over 2,000 people went to his funeral.

[1]cancer (n) a serious disease that makes people very sick because cells in the body grow in ways that are not normal or controlled

126

127

❷ MORE READING

Critical thinking and collaboration

Multiple critical thinking activities prepare students for exercises that focus on academic reading skills. Collaboration activities help develop higher-level thinking skills, oral communication, and understanding of different opinions. By working with others students, they become better prepared for real life social and academic situations.

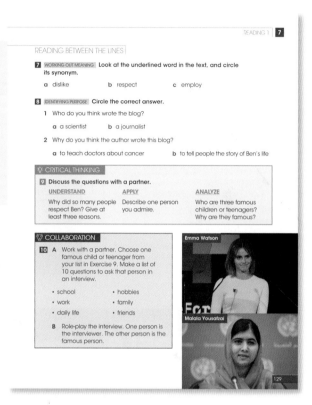

❸ VIDEO

Summarizing the unit

Each unit ends with a carefully selected video clip that piques student interest and pulls together what they have learned. Video lessons also develop key skills such as prediction, comprehension, and discussion.

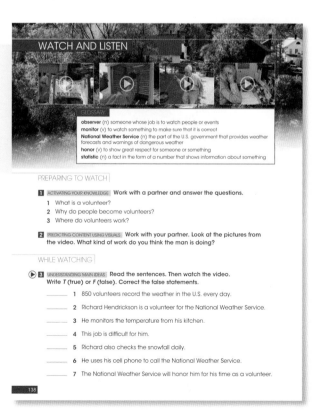

PREPARE YOUR STUDENTS TO SUCCEED IN COLLEGE CLASSES AND BEYOND

Capturing interest

- Students experience the topics and expand their vocabulary through captivating readings and videos that pull together everything they have learned in the unit, while developing academic reading and critical thinking skills.

- Teachers can deliver effective and engaging lessons using Presentation Plus.

Building confidence

- *Prism Reading* teaches skills that enable students to read, understand, and analyze university texts with confidence.

- Readings from a variety of academic disciplines in different formats (essays, articles, websites, etc.) expose and prepare students to comprehend real-life text they may face in or outside the classroom.

Extended learning

- The Online Workbook has one extra reading and additional practice for each unit. Automated feedback gives autonomy to students while allowing teachers to spend less time grading and more time teaching.

Research-based

- Topics, vocabulary, academic and critical thinking skills to build students' confidence and prepare them for college courses were shaped by conversations with teachers at over 500 institutions.

- Carefully selected vocabulary students need to be successful in college are based on the General Service List, the Academic Word List, and the Cambridge English Corpus.

PATH TO
BETTER LEARNING

CLEAR LEARNING OBJECTIVES

Every unit begins with clear learning objectives.

RICH CONTENT

Highly visual unit openers with discussion questions are engaging opportunities for previewing unit themes.

SCAFFOLDED INSTRUCTION

Activities and tasks support the development of critical thinking skills.

COLLABORATIVE GROUP WORK

Critical thinking is followed by collaborative tasks and activities for the opportunity to apply new skills. Tasks are project-based and require teamwork, research, and presentation. These projects are similar to ones in an academic program.

CRITICAL THINKING

After reading, targeted questions help develop critical thinking skills. The questions range in complexity to prepare students for higher-level course work.

EXTENDED LEARNING OPPORTUNITIES

In-class projects and online activities extend learning beyond the textbook.

WHAT MAKES *PRISM READING* SPECIAL: CRITICAL THINKING

BLOOM'S TAXONOMY

Prism Reading prepares students for college coursework by explicitly teaching a full range of critical thinking skills. Critical thinking exercises appear in every unit of every level, organized according to the taxonomy developed by Benjamin Bloom.

Critical thinking exercises are highlighted in a special box and indicates which skills the students are learning.

CRITICAL THINKING

7 SYNTHESIZING **Work with a partner. Use ideas from Reading 1 and Reading 2 to discuss the questions.**

APPLY
Who are the most famous people in your country?

ANALYZE
How can famous people inspire others to do good things?

EVALUATE
Think about the people in Unit 7. Who are you the most similar to? Explain.

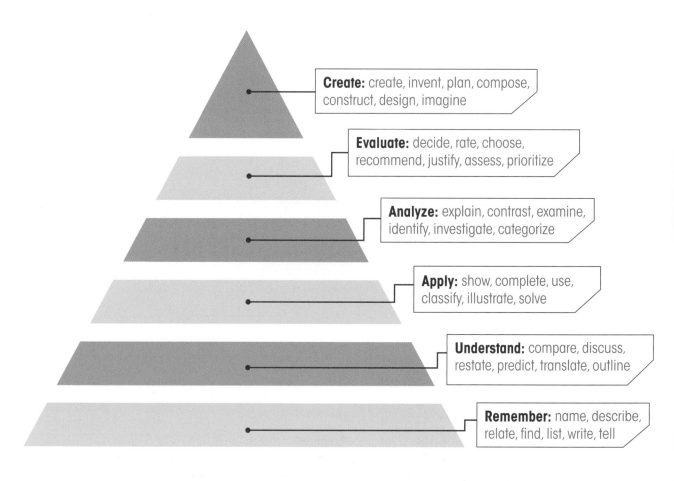

Create: create, invent, plan, compose, construct, design, imagine

Evaluate: decide, rate, choose, recommend, justify, assess, prioritize

Analyze: explain, contrast, examine, identify, investigate, categorize

Apply: show, complete, use, classify, illustrate, solve

Understand: compare, discuss, restate, predict, translate, outline

Remember: name, describe, relate, find, list, write, tell

HIGHER-ORDER THINKING SKILLS

Create, Evaluate, Analyze

Students' academic success depends on their ability to derive knowledge from collected data, make educated judgments, and deliver insightful presentations. *Prism Reading* helps students gain these skills with activities that teach them the best solution to a problem, and develop arguments for a discussion or presentation.

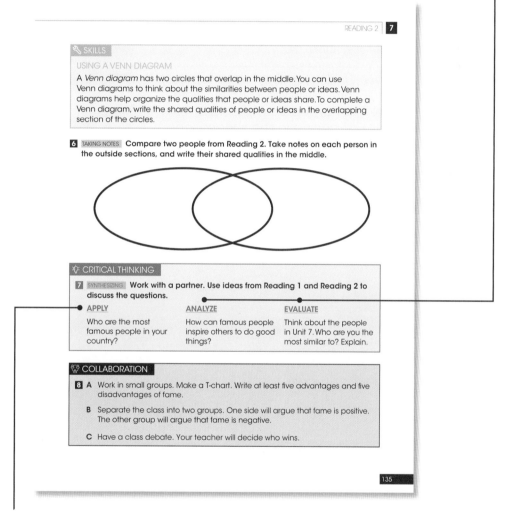

READING 2   **7**

SKILLS

USING A VENN DIAGRAM

A *Venn diagram* has two circles that overlap in the middle. You can use Venn diagrams to think about the similarities between people or ideas. Venn diagrams help organize the qualities that people or ideas share. To complete a Venn diagram, write the shared qualities of people or ideas in the overlapping section of the circles.

6 TAKING NOTES   Compare two people from Reading 2. Take notes on each person in the outside sections, and write their shared qualities in the middle.

CRITICAL THINKING

7 SYNTHESIZING   Work with a partner. Use ideas from Reading 1 and Reading 2 to discuss the questions.

APPLY	ANALYZE	EVALUATE
Who are the most famous people in your country?	How can famous people inspire others to do good things?	Think about the people in Unit 7. Who are you the most similar to? Explain.

COLLABORATION

8 **A** Work in small groups. Make a T-chart. Write at least five advantages and five disadvantages of fame.

   B Separate the class into two groups. One side will argue that fame is positive. The other group will argue that fame is negative.

   C Have a class debate. Your teacher will decide who wins.

135

LOWER-ORDER THINKING SKILLS

Apply, Understand, Remember

Students need to be able to recall information, comprehend it, and see its use in new contexts. These skills form the foundation for all higher-order thinking, and *Prism Reading* develops them through exercises that teach note-taking, comprehension, and the ability to distill information from charts.

PLACES

LEARNING OBJECTIVES

Key Reading Skills	Scanning for numbers; using a T-chart
Additional Reading Skills	Understanding key vocabulary; previewing; reading for main ideas; reading for details; scanning to find information; working out meaning; scanning to predict content; taking notes; making inferences; synthesizing
Language Development	Nouns, verbs, and adjectives

ACTIVATE YOUR KNOWLEDGE

Look at the photo and answer the questions.

1   Where is the place in the photo? Is it in the city or in the country?

2   Is it similar to or different from the place where you live? How?

3   Would you like to live here? Why or why not?

PREPARING TO READ

1 UNDERSTANDING KEY VOCABULARY **You are going to read a report about cities. Read the sentences. Write the words in bold next to the definitions on page 17.**

1　More than 8 million people live in New York City. New York City has the largest **population** in the United States.

2　The city hired an **expert** to help decide on the best place for the new shopping mall. He knows a lot about planning big cities.

3　People who live in big cities often visit the **countryside** so they can get away from the crowds and breathe some fresh air.

4　Studying in another country gives students the **opportunity** to learn about new cultures and see how other people live.

5　The sky was so gray with air **pollution** from cars and factory smoke that I couldn't see the sunset.

6　Shanghai is thousands of years old, but it is also a very **modern** city. It is filled with tall glass buildings and bright lights.

7　Big cities usually have a lot of **traffic**, especially when people drive to work in the morning and drive home in the evening.

8　Washington, D.C., is the **capital** of the United States. It is where the U.S. government is run.

a _____ (n) the cars, trucks, and other vehicles using a road

b _____ (n) land that is not in towns or cities and may have farms and fields

c _____ (adj) designed and made using the most recent ideas and methods

d _____ (n) the number of people living in a place

e _____ (n) damage caused to water, air, and land by harmful materials or waste

f _____ (n) the most important city in a country or state; where the government is

g _____ (n) someone who has a lot of skill in or a lot of knowledge about something

h _____ (n) a chance to do or experience something good

2 PREVIEWING **Look at the title, subheadings, photos, and infographic in the report on pages 18–19. Then answer the questions.**

1 What does *mega* mean?

   a very busy   b very good   c very big

2 Are there more or fewer megacities today than in the past? _____

3 Which city has the most people?

   a Cairo   b Delhi   c Tokyo

3 **After you read the report, check your answers to Exercise 2.**

RISE OF THE MEGACITIES

CITIES GET BIGGER AND PEOPLE GET CLOSER

> " Today, more than 35 cities in the world are megacities.

1 Megacities are defined as cities with more than ten million people. The number of megacities is growing very quickly. In the 1950s, there were only two megacities in the world.

2 Today, 12% of the world's urban[1] **population** lives in megacities. Studies show that there will be eight billion people in the world in 2025. **Experts** say that there will be 40 megacities.

3 Today, more than 35 cities in the world are megacities. 75% are in Asia, South America, and Africa. More and more people around the world are leaving their homes in the **countryside** and moving to the city.

4 Many megacities have better **opportunities**, such as more jobs and a choice of schools and universities.

Megacities are also exciting places to live—there are lots of different people, languages, and restaurants, and there are many interesting things to do.

5 However, megacities have problems, too. The cities are very big, and this can cause problems like **pollution** or poor housing[2].

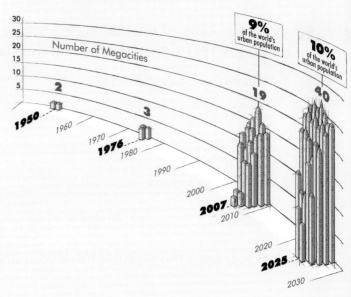

Number of Megacities

9% of the world's urban population

10% of the world's urban population

1950 — 2
1960
1970
1976 — 3
1980
1990
2000
2007 — 19
2010
2020
2025 — 40
2030

TOKYO, JAPAN ▶
37.8 MILLION

6 Tokyo is an exciting **modern** city in the east of Japan. There are lots of jobs because most big companies in Japan are in Tokyo. It is also an excellent place to study—20% of Japan's universities are in the city. However, Tokyo is very busy, and the **traffic** is very bad. More than 8.7 million people use the subway every day.

◀DELHI, INDIA
25 MILLION

7 Delhi is in the north of India. It has many beautiful monuments[3], interesting museums, and modern restaurants. There is an exciting mix of different cultures in the city, and there are four official languages: Hindi, Urdu, Punjabi, and English. However, there are not enough houses in some parts of Delhi. This means that many people live in large <u>slums</u> in the city.

CAIRO, EGYPT ▶
16.9 MILLION

8 Cairo is the **capital** of Egypt, and it is the largest city in Africa. Cairo has important car and film industries. The city is the center of many government offices and has many universities, one of which is over 1,200 years old.

[1]urban (adj) relating to towns and cities

[2]housing (n) places to live, such as apartments or houses

[3]monuments (n) old buildings or places that are important in history

4 READING FOR MAIN IDEAS **Read the report on pages 18–19. Write *T* (true) or *F* (false) next to the statements. Then correct the false sentences.**

_____ 1 There are more megacities now than in 1950.

_____ 2 There are many opportunities to study in megacities.

_____ 3 Many people leave the countryside and move to a city.

_____ 4 Almost 35 cities in the world are megacities.

_____ 5 Most megacities are in Europe.

_____ 6 Finding a house or an apartment to live in is easy in megacities.

5 READING FOR DETAILS **Read the report again. Write the words in the correct place in the table. Some words may fit in more than one place.**

| mix of different people   interesting places to visit |
| lots of jobs   traffic   good place to study   housing problem |
| important industries   busy trains |

Tokyo	
Delhi	
Cairo	

🔧 SKILLS

SCANNING FOR NUMBERS

When scanning a text, readers look for specific information and details. Do not read the whole text. Readers often scan a text to find important numbers, percentages, and dates.

6 SCANNING TO FIND INFORMATION **Find and circle all the numbers in the report on pages 18–19. Then complete the student's notes with the correct numbers.**

1 number of megacities in 1950 = _____
2 predicted number of megacities in 2025 = _____
3 percent of urban population in the world that live in
   megacities = _____ %
4 expected global population in 2025 = _____ billion
5 number of people who use the subway in Tokyo = _____ million
6 percent of Japanese universities in Tokyo = _____ %
7 number of people living in Delhi = _____ million
8 number of official languages spoken in Delhi = _____
9 age of Cairo's oldest university = over _____ years old

READING BETWEEN THE LINES

7 WORKING OUT MEANING **Look at the word *slums* underlined in the report. What do you think it means? Circle the correct answer.**

a   a very poor and crowded area in a city
b   a very unclean house
c   a very expensive area in the center of a city

☀ CRITICAL THINKING

8 **Work with a partner. Discuss the questions.**

APPLY	ANALYZE	EVALUATE
Are there any megacities in or near your country?	Why are modern cities growing so quickly?	What are the best solutions to pollution and poor housing?

😯 COLLABORATION

9 **A**   Work in small groups. Number each group in the class 1 or 2.

• Group 1 - Make a list of 5-10 good things about living in a city.

• Group 2 - Make a list of 5-10 bad things about living in a city.

B   As a class, combine your lists on the board. Then vote for the top 5 things in each list.

1 UNDERSTANDING KEY VOCABULARY **Read the definitions. Complete the sentences with the correct form of the words in bold.**

> **area** (n) a region or part of a larger place, like a country or city
> **cheap** (adj) not expensive, or costs less than usual
> **downtown** (adj) the main or central part of a city
> **expensive** (adj) costs a lot of money; not cheap
> **local** (adj) relating to a particular area, city, or town
> **noisy** (adj) loud; makes a lot of noise
> **quiet** (adj) makes little or no noise

1 My hotel is _____ and calm. It is outside of the busy city center, so it isn't loud at night.

2 Central Park is a nice _____ to relax in New York City.

3 When people visit new cities, it's a good idea to ask _____ people for the best restaurants. They know the most about their city.

4 Since the airline was new, they offered _____ flights from New York City to Boston. A lot of new customers bought tickets at low prices.

Chicago, Illinois

5 We took the bus to _____ Chicago because that is where the main tourist sites in the city are located.

6 It's getting more _____ to live in a big city, so people who can't pay the high prices are moving away.

7 There was a lot of traffic on my street last night. There were so many

_____, loud cars that I couldn't sleep.

2 SCANNING TO PREDICT CONTENT   **Read the title of the article on page 24. What general topic do you think the article is about?**

a geography   **b** tourism   **c** history

3 **Read paragraph 1 and check your answer.**

4 **Find the words in paragraph 1 that tell you the answer. Then write the words in the blanks.**

_____

_____

_____

HOMESTAY VACATIONS
A HOME AWAY FROM HOME

1 Homestays are becoming more and more popular, and people around the world are offering their homes as hotels. Homestays offer **cheap** places to stay and the chance for guests to see the **area** like **local** people. They are very popular with students who want to stay in another country and learn a language. We asked three families who run homestays to tell us about where they live.

THE ATAL FAMILY

2 Our family home is in the north of Nepal, in the Himalayan Mountains, in the village of Manang. The village[1] is small and very **quiet**. It is a very friendly place. The mountains are extremely beautiful. You can go for long walks and swim in the rivers, but there are no stores, movie theaters, or cafés.

Manang, Nepal

[1] **village** (n) a very small town in the countryside

Washington, United States

KATE AND JULIAN FOXTON

3 Our two-bedroom house is in Washington State, in the U.S. It is in the Pacific Northwest. It is a 20-minute drive to the nearest city, Seattle. There are a lot of lakes, rivers, and forests, and it is very quiet. We spend a lot of time reading books, watching movies, and going for walks in the forest, where we see a lot of flowers and small animals. Our area is great for sports like hiking, kayaking, and mountain biking. However, the houses here are **expensive**, which can be a problem for local people. There aren't many buses or trains here, so it can be difficult to get around without a car.

CHAFIC AND ALINE HALWANY

4 Our home is near the historic **downtown** area of Beirut, Lebanon, one of the largest cities in the Middle East. There are lots of cafés and restaurants, which are open late at night. We love it here because it's so friendly and you can always find what you need – lots of people come to learn Arabic and French. There are also a lot of jobs and businesses here. However, it can be **noisy** at night, and there is a lot of traffic during the day. The best thing about Beirut is the weather. It is nice all year round; it rains in the winter, but there is no snow.

Beirut, Lebanon

5 READING FOR MAIN IDEAS **Read the text on pages 24–25. Write the headings above the matching paragraphs in the article.**

A Big City   A Mountain Village   A House near the Forest

6 READING FOR DETAILS **Look at the summaries of the paragraphs. Cross out the incorrect words in bold and write the correct words. The first one has been done for you as an example.**

1   The Atal family lives in a *village* ~~**city**~~. It is a **busy** place. The mountains are very **cold**.

2   Kate and Julian Foxton live in the **Northeast** of the United States.

    The area is great for **theaters**. The houses are really **cheap**.

3   Chafic and Aline Halwany live in a **small** city. People learn **English** and

    French in the downtown area. There is a lot of traffic **at night**.

> ✎ SKILLS
>
> USING A T-CHART
> You can use a T-chart to write about positives (+) and negatives (–). Write about the positives in one column and the negatives in the other column.

7 TAKING NOTES **What are the positives and negatives of living in the places you read about? Complete the T-chart with your notes about Manang. Then make two more T-charts in your notebook about Washington and Beirut.**

positive (+)	negative (–)

READING BETWEEN THE LINES

8 MAKING INFERENCES **Work with a partner.
Discuss the questions.**

1 Why are homestays cheap places to stay?
2 How many languages do the Halwanys speak?
3 Do Kate and Julian have children?

☼ CRITICAL THINKING

9 SYNTHESIZING **Work with a partner. Use ideas from Reading 1 and Reading 2 to answer the questions.**

UNDERSTAND	ANALYZE	EVALUATE
Choose one city or family you read about, and summarize the ideas.	Why do young people leave the countryside to live in the city?	Think of a large city that you know. What do local people and tourists there do for fun in large cities? Do you think they do the same things?

⚙ COLLABORATION

10 **A** Work with a partner. Describe your hometown or city. Describe the kind of person who lives there. Take notes on what your partner says.

B Change partners. Use your notes, and summarize your first partner's descriptions to your new partner. Again, take notes on what your partner says.

C Compare the summaries in step B with the descriptions in step A. Are they the same or different?

LANGUAGE DEVELOPMENT

NOUNS, VERBS, AND ADJECTIVES

A *noun* refers to a person, place, or thing. **girl**
A *verb* describes an action. **run**
An *adjective* describes a noun. **tall**

noun	*verb*			*adjective*	*adjective*	*noun*		*noun*	
Jenny	**swam**	in the		**warm**	**blue**	**sea**	on her	**vacation**	last year.

1 Look at the sentence and the numbered words. Match the numbers to the parts of speech.

> (1) Delhi (2) has many (3) beautiful (1) monuments,
>
> (3) interesting (1) museums, and (3) modern (1) restaurants.
>
> noun _____
>
> verb _____
>
> adjective _____

2 Write the words from the box in the correct places in the table.

> live   town   excellent   drive   exciting
> have   café   different   building

noun	verb	adjective

LANGUAGE

Adjectives describe nouns. Use the structure *adjective + noun*.

	adjective	+	noun
Beirut is an	**interesting**		**city**.
There are many	**excellent**		**restaurants**.

Adjectives are never plural.

a different place → some ~~differents~~ places → some different places

---

3 **Match the adjectives to their opposites.**

1	interesting	a	expensive
2	cheap	b	boring
3	polluted	c	clean
4	beautiful	d	quiet
5	noisy	e	ugly

4 **Complete the sentences with adjectives from Exercise 3.**

1 There are lots of cars and traffic jams. The air is very _____.

2 This is a(n) _____ city. Everything costs a lot of money.

3 My town is very _____. There isn't any noise.

4 Chicago is a really _____ place. There are lots of things to do.

5 The building looks horrible. It's very _____.

WATCH AND LISTEN

GLOSSARY

beat out (phr v) to win something in a competition that someone else wants

Civil War (n) the war between the North (the Union) and the South (the Confederacy) in the United States from 1861 to 1865, which was won by the North

cuisine (n) a style of cooking

draw (n) something that people want to see or visit

regulate (v) to control an activity or process by rules or a system

tourism (n) the business of providing services for tourists

PREPARING TO WATCH

1 ACTIVATING YOUR KNOWLEDGE **Work with a partner and answer the questions.**

1 What makes a city beautiful?

2 Why might a city win an award?

3 Have you ever visited a beautiful city? If so, describe it.

2 PREDICTING CONTENT USING VISUALS **You are going to watch a video about a city that won an award. Read the heading in the box and look at the pictures from the video. Then discuss the questions with your partner.**

> "And the award for top U.S. city goes to ..."

1 What city do you think won the award?

2 Why do you think the city won the award?

WHILE WATCHING

▶ **3** UNDERSTANDING DETAILS **Watch the video. Then circle the correct answers.**

1 Charleston won against another city named *San Francisco* / *San Diego*.

2 This other city won the award for *13* / *18* years in a row.

3 People are *surprised* / *not surprised* when they come to Charleston.

4 The tourism industry in Charleston is *not regulated* / *regulated*.

5 More than three *million* / *billion* dollars are brought in by visitors a year.

▶ **4** UNDERSTANDING MAIN IDEAS **Watch again and match the questions to the answers.**

1   What is Charleston called?

2   Who is Joe Riley?

3   What can you feel all around Charleston?

4   What do people sell in the market?

5   What things are regulated?

a   buses and walking tours

b   "the Holy City"

c   the history

d   the mayor

e   handmade crafts

5 MAKING INFERENCES **Work with a partner. Discuss the meanings of the underlined words from the video.**

1   Charleston's many church <u>steeples</u> reach high into the sky.

2   Some of its houses were built two or three hundred years ago. They are two or three <u>centuries</u> old.

3   Tourists buy souvenirs from <u>vendors</u> in the city market.

4   In Charleston, tourists often ride in horse <u>carriages</u> instead of cars.

☼ CRITICAL THINKING

6 **Work with a partner. Discuss the questions.**

REMEMBER	ANALYZE	EVALUATE
Think of one scene from the video and describe it to your group.	Would you like to visit Charleston? Why or why not?	Choose one city from Unit 1. Compare it to your hometown.

☙ COLLABORATION

7 **A**   Work in small groups. Imagine you are entering a contest for "Best Hometown." Choose a town or city that you know. Prepare a group presentation. Include:

• a short introduction and history

• the 5-10 best tourist attractions

• a 30-second speech about why your town should win

B   Give your presentation to the class. As a class, vote for the best hometown.

UNIT 2

FESTIVALS AND CELEBRATIONS

LEARNING OBJECTIVES

Key Reading Skill	Previewing
Additional Reading Skills	Understanding key vocabulary; using your knowledge; taking notes; reading for details; recognizing text type; scanning to predict content; reading for main ideas; making inferences; synthesizing
Language Development	Prepositions of time and place; adverbs of frequency

ACTIVATE YOUR KNOWLEDGE

Work with a partner. Look at the photos and discuss the questions.

1 What is happening in the large photo?

2 What is happening in the small photos?

3 What countries do you think the photos are from?

READING 1

1 UNDERSTANDING KEY VOCABULARY **Read the definitions. Complete the sentences with the correct form of the words in bold.**

> **celebrate** (v) to do something enjoyable because it is a special day
> **culture** (n) the habits, traditions, and beliefs of a country or group of people
> **gift** (n) something that you give to someone, usually on a special day
> **the ground** (n) the surface of the Earth
> **lucky** (adj) having good things happen to you
> **traditional** (adj) following the ways of behaving or doing things that have continued in a group of people for a long time

1 I always _____ my mother's birthday by making a big meal for our family. She loves to see everyone get together for a special day.

2 There are a lot of festivals in Korean _____. Each one has special food and events.

3 In Japan, guests usually give a small wrapped _____, like cake or fruit, when they visit someone's home.

4 For our International Day party, all of my classmates wore _____ clothing from their countries instead of their usual clothes.

5 In many countries, people believe the color yellow is _____. Wearing yellow will bring you good things like joy and energy.

6 On Arbor Day in the U.S., a lot of people dig holes and plant new trees in _____.

⚒ SKILLS

PREVIEWING

Before you read, look at the photos, title, and subtitles. This gives you a lot of information about the topic of the text before you read. It will help you understand the text better when you read it.

2 PREVIEWING Look at the photos, title, and subtitles in the article on pages 36–37. Circle the topic of the article. After you read the article, check your answer.

a celebrations around the world

b weddings around the world

c birthdays around the world

3 USING YOUR KNOWLEDGE Write five family celebrations and five national festivals or celebrations in the chart.

FAMILY CELEBRATIONS	NATIONAL CELEBRATIONS

Hot Air Balloon Festival in Albuquerque, NM

CELEBRATE!

People **celebrate** special days in different ways around the world. These celebrations are an important part of their **culture**. Let's take a look at five examples.

Piñatas

In Mexico, children often have piñatas on their birthday. The child's parents put chocolates and other candy inside the piñata and hang it on a tree. Then the children hit the piñata with a stick. It breaks, and the candy falls out onto **the ground**.

Piñatas

Noodles

In China, people celebrate weddings with an eight-course meal because the word *eight* sounds like the word for *good luck*. The last dish of the meal is always noodles. The noodles are long and thin. You have to eat them in one piece—you can't cut them. In Chinese culture, long noodles are **lucky**. Long noodles mean you will have a long life.

Noodles

Mother's Day

4 Many people around the world honor their mothers on Mother's Day. In the U.S., Mother's Day is always celebrated on the second Sunday in May. Sons and daughters like to give their mother a day to rest, so they might surprise her by cleaning the house or cooking a nice meal for her. They also give her **gifts** such as flowers or jewelry. Many families take their mother to a restaurant for lunch or dinner.

Mother's Day

Name Days

5 As well as a birthday, many people in southern Europe also celebrate their name day. In Greece, name days are more important than birthdays. People have big parties and open their houses to anybody who wants to come. People bring small gifts, often flowers or a box of candy.

Name Days

Coming of Age Day

6 In Japan, people celebrate Coming of Age Day, or *Seijin no hi*, on the second Monday in January. On this holiday, Japan congratulates people who have turned 20 years old between April 2 of the last year to April 1 of the current year. In Japanese culture, this is the age when teenagers become adults and take on the responsibilities of being an adult. Young women usually wear a **traditional** *furisode* kimono, while young men often wear Western style suits, and they attend a ceremony[1] in their area. They receive small gifts and celebrate with their friends after the ceremony.

[1]ceremony (n) a formal event that people go to, often for a holiday or to celebrate someone or something

Coming of Age Day

4 TAKING NOTES **Read the article on pages 36–37. Highlight the description of each celebration below in the article. Write the name of the country in the chart.**

country	description of celebration
(1)	use a stick to get candy
(2)	eat long noodles
(3)	more important than a birthday
(4)	wear traditional clothes
(5)	second Sunday in May

5 READING FOR DETAILS **Read the article again and write *T* (true) or *F* (false) next to the statements. Then correct the false statements.**

_____ **1** Piñatas have flowers inside them.

_____ **2** Long noodles are unlucky in Chinese culture.

_____ **3** Mother's Day in the U.S. is the first week in May.

_____ **4** On name days, people bring gifts.

_____ **5** On Coming of Age Day, people wear special clothes.

READING BETWEEN THE LINES

6 RECOGNIZING TEXT TYPE **Where would you find this article? Circle the correct answer.**

a in a magazine
b in an academic journal

7 **Circle the features that helped you find the answer to Exercise 6.**

photos	color of text	length of paragraphs	title
	number of paragraphs	design of the article	

☼ CRITICAL THINKING

8 **Work with a partner. Discuss the questions.**

APPLY

What special days do you celebrate?

APPLY

What do you do on these days?

ANALYZE

Choose an event in Reading 1. Do you celebrate it similarly or differently?

🐾 COLLABORATION

9 **A** Work in a small group. Choose a holiday. Brainstorm words and ideas about the holiday in the idea map.

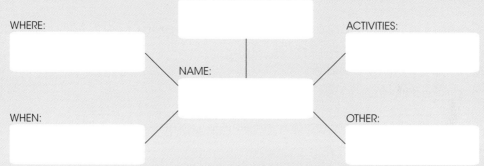

FOOD & DRINKS:

WHERE:

ACTIVITIES:

NAME:

WHEN:

OTHER:

B Share your idea map with another group. Ask and answer questions.

C Give a short presentation about the holiday to the class. Use your idea map to organize your presentation. Include photos or other visuals.

A young woman celebrates her 15th birthday in Mexico.

READING 2

 1 UNDERSTANDING KEY VOCABULARY **You are going to read about the Muscat Festival in Oman. Read the sentences. Circle the best definition for the words or phrases in bold.**

1 The children enjoyed a lot of **activities** at the birthday party. They had their faces painted, played games, and pet different animals.

  a things people do for fun

  b things people say

2 The end of the Civil War is an important day in U.S. **history**.

  a events that are happening now

  b the whole series of events in the past that relate to the development of a country, subject, or person

3 Carnival in Rio de Janeiro, Brazil, is a very **popular** event. Millions of people watch the parades for several days.

  a liked by many people

  b disliked by many people

4 The **highlight** of every holiday is getting together with loved ones.

  a location

  b most enjoyable part

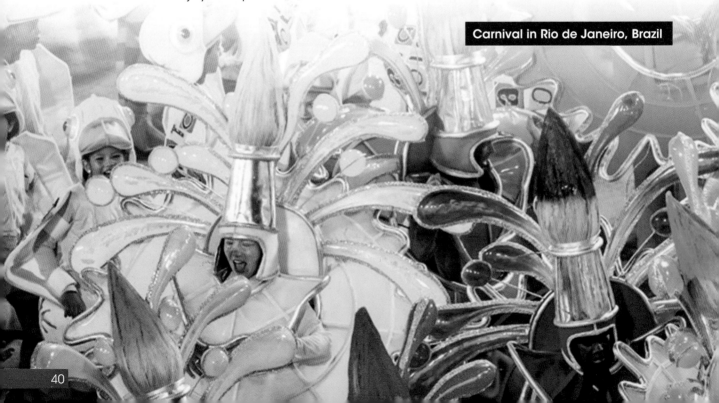

Carnival in Rio de Janeiro, Brazil

5 Nearly everyone in town **takes part in** the race. There is a shorter race for children and a longer one for adults.

   a does an activity with other people

   b eats special types of food

6 Thousands of **visitors** went to the museum on the first day it opened.

   a does an activity with other people

   b eats special types of food

LANGUAGE

Proper nouns are names of people, countries, cities, festivals, and nationalities. Days of the week and months are also proper nouns.

---

2   SCANNING TO PREDICT CONTENT   **Read paragraph 1 in the text on page 42 and circle the proper nouns. Then write them in the box. Scan the other paragraphs. Add at least 10 more proper nouns.**

MUSCAT FESTIVAL

A CELEBRATION OF OMANI CULTURE

1 One of the most important festivals in Oman is the Muscat Festival. The festival lasts for about one month and takes place in February every year. During the festival, many **activities** are available for people to **take part in**.

2 Large numbers of people, including local Omanis and **visitors** to Oman, go to the different events. The events are a celebration of both Omani and international **history** and traditions. The events take place in different places across the country. Many businesses show their products for people to look at and buy.

Omani girls

3   The Muscat Festival also includes the very **popular** six-day Tour of Oman bike race. Professional cyclists from around the world take part in the race. The race is 620 miles (1,000 kilometers) long, and it takes the cyclists up the beautiful Jabal Al Akhdhar— the Green Mountain.

4   Other **highlights** of the Muscat Festival include the chance to try out different types of food at the Oman Food Festival. The Muscat Art Festival also offers Arabic music, concerts and plays, and other entertainment for the whole family. The Festival of Lights is one of the most popular events at the Muscat Festival.

5   The Muscat Festival is an international event, with people visiting from countries as far away as Brazil and Cuba. Visitors also arrive from Italy, India, Russia, South Korea, Spain, Tunisia, and Turkey, as well as many other countries. They enjoy the amazing clothes, food, and music. Some people just enjoy the mix of different cultures.

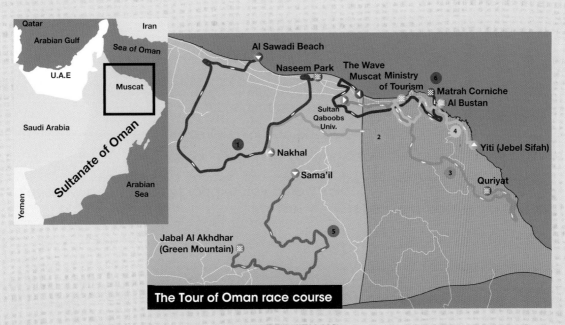
The Tour of Oman race course

CONNECT WITH US

3 READING FOR MAIN IDEAS **Read the text on pages 42–43. Write the paragraph number next to the ideas. Underline the information in the text that helped you find the answer.**

a   the countries people visit from   Paragraph _____

b   how long the Muscat Festival lasts   Paragraph _____

c   different events in the festival   Paragraph _____

d   international culture   Paragraph _____

e   the Tour of Oman   Paragraph _____

4 READING FOR DETAILS **Read the text again, and complete the sentences.**

1   The Muscat Festival happens in the month of _____ .

2   People from all over the world _____ the festival.

3   The English name for the Jabal Al Akhdhar is the _____ .

4   You can see plays at the _____ .

5   The Festival of Lights is a very _____ event.

6   Visitors enjoy clothes, _____ , and _____ .

READING BETWEEN THE LINES

5 RECOGNIZING TEXT TYPE **Where would you find this text?**

a   on a tourism website describing the culture of Oman

b   on a tourism website describing the economy of Oman

6 MAKING INFERENCES **What other topics would you expect to find on this website? Add two more topics to the list.**

1   places to eat   3   _____

2   things to do   4   _____

☀ CRITICAL THINKING

7 SYNTHESIZING **Work with a partner. Use ideas from Reading 1 and Reading 2 to discuss the questions.**

APPLY

Would you like to visit the countries you read about? Why or why not?

ANALYZE

What information about festivals in your country would you give a visitor?

EVALUATE

Compare the celebrations you read about with other celebrations you know. How are they different?

🐾 COLLABORATION

8 A Work in pairs. Make a list of five festivals or holidays that most people celebrate around the world.

B Take a survey. Ask students to put the festival or holidays on your list in order from most popular to least popular. Which festival or holiday on your list is the most popular in your class? Share your results with the class.

LANGUAGE DEVELOPMENT

PREPOSITIONS OF TIME AND PLACE

LANGUAGE

Use *on* with a specific date or day and with the *weekend / weekends.*

My birthday is **on** May 1 / **on** Saturday. I wake up late **on** weekends.

Use *in* with a month and with *the morning, the afternoon,* and *the evening.*

My birthday is **in** May. We eat breakfast **in** the morning.

Use *in* with a country, city, or town.

We have an apartment **in** France / **in** Paris.

Use *at* with a specific time and with *night.*

We eat dinner **at** seven o'clock **at** night.

Use *at* with *school, work,* and *home.*

We have a party **at** school.

1 Write the words from the box in the correct space in the table.

> school   June   Sunday   home   work   a town
> Istanbul   the evening   the morning   night   January 1
> my country   Brazil   eight o'clock   Tuesday

	on	in	at
places			
times			

2 Complete the sentences with *on, in,* or *at.*

1 People have parties _____ work with their colleagues.

2 We have a big family meal _____ Saturday.

3 The festival is _____ November.

4 My brother's wedding is _____ December 2.

5 The children wake up _____ seven o'clock.

6 People celebrate Thanksgiving _____ the U.S.

7 We stay _____ home for the whole weekend.

8 We eat dinner late _____ night.

9 We meet our friends _____ the weekend.

ADVERBS OF FREQUENCY

LANGUAGE

Use adverbs of frequency to talk about habits. They describe how often someone does something. Adverbs of frequency usually go before the verb.

In Mexico, children **often** have piñatas on their birthday.

In China, my family **always** celebrates weddings with an eight-course meal.

Children in the U.S. **sometimes** clean the house on Mother's Day.

During Eid, people **usually** visit family and friends.

My family **never** cuts their noodles at a wedding in China.

0%				100%
never	sometimes	often	usually	always

3 **Complete the sentences with adverbs of frequency that are true for you. Compare your answers with a partner.**

1 I _____ visit my parents on the holidays.

2 I _____ give my friends a present on their birthday.

3 I _____ celebrate New Year's Eve.

4 I _____ go to weddings.

5 I _____ eat candy on special occasions.

WATCH AND LISTEN

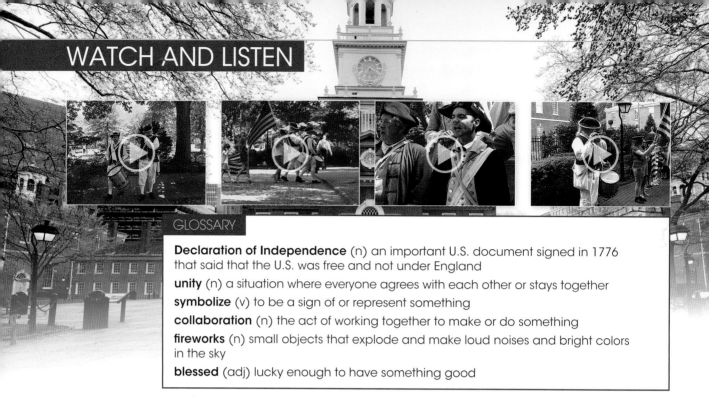

GLOSSARY

Declaration of Independence (n) an important U.S. document signed in 1776 that said that the U.S. was free and not under England

unity (n) a situation where everyone agrees with each other or stays together

symbolize (v) to be a sign of or represent something

collaboration (n) the act of working together to make or do something

fireworks (n) small objects that explode and make loud noises and bright colors in the sky

blessed (adj) lucky enough to have something good

PREPARING TO WATCH

1 ACTIVATING YOUR KNOWLEDGE **Work with a partner and answer the questions.**

1 Is it important to learn about a country's history? Why or why not?

2 What things, like buildings, show a country's history?

3 Why do some people not like learning about history?

2 PREDICTING CONTENT USING VISUALS **You are going to watch a video about an American celebration. Look at the pictures from the video. What are the people doing?**

WHILE WATCHING

▶ 3 UNDERSTANDING DETAILS **Read the words. Then watch the video. Check the things that you see or hear in the video.**

1 ☐ a flag   4 ☐ fireworks   7 ☐ a guitar
2 ☐ a costume   5 ☐ children   8 ☐ old glasses
3 ☐ a drum   6 ☐ a parade

▶ 4 Watch again. Choose the correct answers.

1 The young Americans are talking about _____.

   a Flag Day   b Independence Day

2 The holiday is on _____.

   a July 4   b June 4

3 This celebration is in _____ .

   a Washington, D.C.   **b** Philadelphia

4 The people are celebrating the date the United States _____ .

   a became independent   **b** won a war

5 What do many children like about this day?

   a the fireworks   **b** the costumes

5 UNDERSTANDING MAIN IDEAS **Match the sentence halves to form the ideas of the speakers in the video.**

1	It symbolizes	**a**	to be American.
2	The fireworks	**b**	to celebrate every year.
3	It's a great day	**c**	to live in this country.
4	We are blessed	**d**	the unity of the country.
5	It's an important day for Americans	**e**	are really fun.

☿ CRITICAL THINKING

6 **Work in small groups. Discuss the questions.**

APPLY	APPLY	CREATE
What are some other ways to learn about history?	What are some important dates in your country's history? Why?	Plan a new holiday for your country.

COLLABORATION

7 **A** Work with a partner. Discuss the following topic: *How can festivals and celebrations teach us about a culture?* Think of at least two festivals or holidays. Be ready to explain your answer and to give examples and reasons.

   B Work in groups of four. Have a roundtable discussion about the topic:

   • Sit in a circle. Each pair shares their answers, examples, and reasons for one to two minutes while other students listen and take notes.

   • At the end of the roundtable, students ask and answer questions.

THE INTERNET AND TECHNOLOGY

LEARNING OBJECTIVES

Key Reading Skills	Reading for main ideas; making inferences
Additional Reading Skills	Understanding key vocabulary; scanning to predict content; reading for details; using your knowledge; taking notes; recognizing text type; synthesizing
Language Development	Compound nouns; giving opinions

ACTIVATE YOUR KNOWLEDGE

Look at the photo and answer the questions.

1. Where is the man?

2. What do you think he is doing?

3. How much time do you spend on the Internet every week?

4. What activities do you use the Internet for?

PREPARING TO READ

1 UNDERSTANDING KEY VOCABULARY **Read the sentences and write the words in bold next to the definitions on page 53.**

1 People should always use a **secret** password on their smartphone. This helps to keep their information safe.

2 After I buy the correct **software**, I'll be able to make music and draw pictures on my computer.

3 Sarah has an **interest** in the newest technology, so she always learns about it very quickly.

4 A lot of websites **collect** information about the people who look at them.

5 Shopping websites must have strong **security**. People have to be sure their personal information and credit card numbers are safe.

6 Ahmed likes to **record** his friends when they do something funny. Then he shares the videos online.

7 One **benefit** of tablets is that they are small, so they are easy to take anywhere with you.

8 Many people don't want to pay to use news websites because so much of the news is already **free** online.

Young Truku women in Taiwan spend time online.

a _____ (n) a good or helpful result or effect

b _____ (n) something you enjoy doing or learning about

c _____ (v) to get things from different places and bring them together

d _____ (adj) costing no money

e _____ (n) the things that are done to keep someone or something safe

f _____ (v) to store sounds, pictures, or information on a camera or computer so that they can be used in the future

g _____ (n) programs you use to make a computer do different things

h _____ (adj) not known or seen by other people

2 SCANNING TO PREDICT CONTENT **Before you read, circle the title and subtitle in the text on pages 54–55.**

3 Circle the best description of the topic of the text.
   a the benefits (+) of the Internet
   b the dangers (–) of the Internet
   c why people use the Internet

4 After you read the text, check your answers to Exercise 3.

Maasai warriors in Kenya track lions with GPS technology.

TECH EXPERT TODAY

SOMEONE'S ALWAYS WATCHING YOU ONLINE...

1 **How do they get my information?** Did you know that when you surf the Web, many websites put **secret software** on your computer? The software **collects** a large amount of information about you and sends it to Internet companies. The Internet companies sell it to other businesses. Your personal information can also be gathered from social media sites. There are many ways your information can be used.

2 **What information do they collect and why?** First, companies collect your information. The companies find out where you live, what websites you visit, and what you do online. With this information, they can guess other things about you. For example, they can guess if you are male[1] or female[2], how old you are, and your **interests**. The companies use this information to decide which advertisements are best for you. Two people can go to the same website, but they will see different ads. For example, someone who likes sports could see an ad for sneakers, and someone who likes films might see an ad for a movie.

continue

Who is tracking you?

3 **What do they do with my information?** Your personal information could also be sold. Some companies collect information just so they can sell it to other businesses. A business that collects and sells personal information is called a *data broker*. When data brokers sell your information, a lot of different companies will know your online habits. Then these companies will advertise products or other websites to you.

4 **What online habits are tracked?** Another way your personal information can be collected is through social media. When your information is on social media, a lot of people can see it. Even if you don't use social media, a friend might post a picture or video of you with your name on it. Pictures and videos can be shared for **free** on social media, which is one of the great **benefits**. However, that same act of sharing could be a problem for your own **security**. If someone knows too much about you, they can steal your identity. Then they can buy things online and post messages while pretending to be you.

5 **Conclusion** All of your online habits can be **recorded**. Studying people's online habits is big business. Your personal information is very valuable to companies. That is how they know who to send their ads to. The Internet reaches almost every corner of the world, but the danger is that your personal information might travel that far, too.

find out more

[1]**male** (adj) a man

[2]**female** (adj) a woman

SKILLS

READING FOR MAIN IDEAS

When reading, it is important to understand the main ideas in the text. Remember that each paragraph has one topic. The main idea of a paragraph is the most important point of what the author says about the topic. The main idea can often be found in the topic sentence, which is usually the first or second sentence in the paragraph.

5 READING FOR MAIN IDEAS **Read the text on pages 54–55. Circle the correct ending for each sentence.**

1 Internet companies *ask you for information / take information without asking you.*

2 Internet companies show *different advertisements to different people / the same advertisements to everyone.*

6 READING FOR DETAILS **Write the words from the box in the correct place in the table. For some items, more than one answer is possible.**

> your address   your interests   your social media page
> other websites you might like   your online habits   your gender (male/female)
> a data broker   your age   the websites you visit

A What do Internet companies find out about you?	B What do Internet companies guess about you?	C What do Internet companies decide?	D How do Internet companies find out about you?

READING BETWEEN THE LINES

⚒ SKILLS

MAKING INFERENCES

When people read, they often make inferences. To make an inference, think about what the author writes, the way they write it, and what you already know about the subject to guess about information not in the text. Inferences are not facts, so different answers are possible.

 7 MAKING INFERENCES **Look at the Internet ads in Reading 1. What can you guess about the person using the website? Discuss the questions with a partner.**

1 How old is the reader?   2 What are the reader's interests?

8 **What can you infer from the text? Circle the correct answers.**

a You can ask companies to stop selling your information.

b You don't know what websites are collecting information about you.

c You should be extra careful with your personal information when you travel.

d Someone could pretend to be you and send an email to your friend.

◌ CRITICAL THINKING

9 **Work with a partner. Discuss the questions.**

APPLY

Describe the last online ad you saw. Did it surprise you?

ANALYZE

Read the three opinions. Which one do you most agree with? Why?

a I don't think companies should take any of your information. Think about the danger of them knowing your private info.

b I don't see the problem. Companies need to make money. We get a lot of free things on the Internet, and it's a good way to pay for them.

c I think it's great. If companies can show you ads for things you like, you can find out about new things.

🤝 COLLABORATION

10 **A** Find someone who shares your opinion in Exercise 9. Now support a different opinion. Make a list of three reasons why your first opinion is wrong.

B Share your reasons with a group who had the opinion you are now supporting. Are they the same or different? Did your real opinion change?

PREPARING TO READ

 1 UNDERSTANDING KEY VOCABULARY **Read the definitions. Complete the sentences with the correct form of the words in bold.**

> **affect** (v) to influence someone or something; to cause change
>
> **creative** (adj) good at thinking of new ideas or creating new and unusual things
>
> **download** (v) to copy computer programs, music, or other information electronically from the Internet to your computer
>
> **educational** (adj) providing education, or relating to education
>
> **imagination** (n) the part of your mind that creates ideas or pictures of things that are not real or that you have not seen
>
> **improve** (v) to get better or to make something better

1   There are a lot of apps you can _____ onto your phone to help you learn a new language.

2   I like to watch _____ videos so I can learn something new. I just watched one about the history of airplanes.

3   Gabriela took a class to _____ her computer skills. Now she can type faster and find information on the Internet more easily.

4   Reading, telling stories, and having new adventures can help kids to develop their _____ .

5 Art students are very _____ . In my program, they use new software to make some really interesting and beautiful designs.

6 Spending too much time on your smartphone may _____ your health in negative ways. It can hurt your eyes and give you a headache.

2 USING YOUR KNOWLEDGE **Discuss the questions with a partner.**

1 Why do some people like video games?

2 What ages do you think most video game players are?

3 USING YOUR KNOWLEDGE **Write the words from the box in the correct place in the table. Then add any synonyms you know to the correct column.**

advantage ~~bad~~ benefit disadvantage ~~good~~ negative positive problem

+	−
good	bad

VIDEO GAMES FOR KIDS: WIN, LOSE, OR DRAW?

1 Do video games **affect** our children negatively? Today, our children spend more and more time online. Many children spend a lot of their free time playing games on the Internet, on video game systems, or on their mobile devices. In the U.S., 97% of teenagers play video games every week, and children as young as five play video games regularly. This information tells us that the benefits and dangers of video games must be carefully considered.

> **Games can help children think creatively.**

2 For many people, video games are fun and **educational**. They have bright lights, funny cartoons, and exciting stories. Everywhere you look, you can see children playing these games. They play on buses and trains, in restaurants, and even at school. Video games also make you think in a **creative** way, and you have to move your hands and eyes quickly. This can **improve** the way that a child's brain works. Video games also make children use their **imagination**. The player has to do many creative things, like draw, tell stories, and build things. Video games are also a good way to teach children about technology because they can learn how computers and other devices work while they play.

3 However, a recent study suggests that video games can also be bad for children. First, children can **download** many games for free. They do not need money, so they do not need to ask their parents if they can download the games. This means that parents often do not know if their children are playing violent or scary games. Second, many children spend too much time playing games on computers, smartphones, and tablets, and this can lead to health problems—children who spend too much time on the computer and do not exercise can become overweight[1]. Third, if children spend too much time playing games instead of doing homework, they can have problems at school and get bad grades. Finally, video games can affect children's social skills. Playing and working with friends is very important for children, and it teaches them how to talk to other people. If children spend too much time playing video games by themselves, they might not learn how to play with their friends.

4 In conclusion, it seems clear that video games have some advantages and some disadvantages. On the one hand, they are fun and have many educational benefits for children. On the other hand, they can cause problems with children's health and social skills. It is up to parents to know what games their children are playing and how much time they spend on them. Parents should also make sure their children get enough exercise and spend time with other children.

[1]overweight (adj) too heavy or weighing more than the normal amount

> " ...video games can affect children's social skills.

4 READING FOR MAIN IDEAS **Read the text on pages 60–61. Write the paragraph numbers that include the main ideas below. Then write the sentences from the text that contain each main idea.**

1   Video games have some disadvantages. Paragraph: _____

Sentence: _____

2   Video games have some advantages. Paragraph: _____

Sentence: _____

5 TAKING NOTES **Find and highlight four more advantages and three more disadvantages of video games in Reading 2, and write them in the T-chart.**

+	−
Video games ... – are creative.	Video games ... – can cause health problems.

READING BETWEEN THE LINES

6 RECOGNIZING TEXT TYPE **Read the questions. Circle the correct answer. Compare your answers with a partner.**

1 What type of text is this?

   a an essay   **b** a newspaper article   **c** a website

2 Who do you think is the author?

   a a parent   **b** a journalist   **c** a student

☼ CRITICAL THINKING

7 SYNTHESIZING **Work with a partner. Use ideas from Reading 1 and Reading 2 to answer the questions.**

ANALYZE	ANALYZE	EVALUATE
Do you think that video games are bad for children? Why or why not?	Is spending a lot of time online good or bad for you?	Describe a time in your life when spending time on the Internet or playing video games was a problem for you.

⚙ COLLABORATION

8 A Work with a partner. Make a survey of 10 questions about people's online habits. Ask three classmates your survey questions. Take notes on their answers.

   B Report the results of your survey to the class. As a class, make five general statements about your online habits.

LANGUAGE DEVELOPMENT

COMPOUND NOUNS

> **LANGUAGE**
>
> In English, two or more words can be put together to form a new word.
>
> A *compound noun* is a noun that is made up of two or three different words. Compound nouns are very common in English. Some compound nouns are written as one word. Others are written as two or three separate words.
>
> A **laptop** is a small computer that you can carry around with you.
>
> A **touch screen** is a screen on a computer, smartphone, or tablet that you touch in order to give it instructions.
>
> A **password** is a secret word that allows you to use your computer.
>
> A **homepage** is the first page you see when you look at the Internet.

1 **Match the compound nouns to their definitions.**

1	video game	**a**	a page of information on the Internet
2	computer program	**b**	a set of keys that you use to type
3	keyboard	**c**	a phone that can be used as a computer
4	email address	**d**	a game that is played on a screen
5	Web page	**e**	instructions that make a computer do something
6	smartphone	**f**	an address for an email inbox

2 **Use the compound nouns from Exercise 1 to complete the sentences.**

1 My computer's _____ is broken. I can only type in capital letters.

2 I just bought a new _____ . I can use the Internet anywhere now.

3 What's your _____ ? I'll send you the pictures from the party.

4 I found a(n) _____ with good information I can use for my essay.

5 I can play this _____ on my computer or on my smartphone.

6 I downloaded a(n) _____ to check my computer for viruses.

GIVING OPINIONS

> ### LANGUAGE
>
> In academic writing, use the phrases *I think that, I believe that, It seems to me that,* and *In my opinion* to talk about your opinions.
>
> Opinion: *Video games are bad for children.*
>
> I **think that** video games are bad for children.
>
> I **believe that** video games are bad for children.
>
> It **seems to me that** video games are bad for children.
>
> **In my opinion,** video games are bad for children.

3 Look at the phrases for giving opinions. Which phrase needs a comma at the end of it?

   a I think that   **c** It seems to me that

   b I believe that   **d** In my opinion

4 Complete the sentences with an adjective. Write sentences that are true for you.

   1 Video games are _____ .

   2 Online shopping is _____ .

   3 Social media sites are _____ .

   4 Online banking is _____ .

   5 Smartphones are _____ .

   6 Watching videos online is _____ .

5 Rewrite the sentences in Exercise 4 to show that they are your opinion. Use the phrases in the box above.

   1 _____

   2 _____

   3 _____

   4 _____

   5 _____

   6 _____

WATCH AND LISTEN

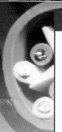

GLOSSARY

habit (n) something that you do regularly, almost without thinking about it

advertising (n) the business of trying to persuade people to buy products or services

ad (n) an advertisement; a picture, short video, song, etc. that tries to get you to buy a product or service

predict (v) to say what you think will happen in the future

clue (n) a sign or piece of information that helps you solve a problem or answer a question

PREPARING TO WATCH

1 ACTIVATING YOUR KNOWLEDGE **Work with a partner and answer the questions.**

1 Why do people buy things from websites?

2 What kind of advertisements or commercials do you see online?

3 Do you ever worry when you use technology? Why or why not?

WHILE WATCHING

2 UNDERSTANDING DETAILS **Watch the video. Complete each sentence with a word from the box.**

| looking taking talking texting showing walking |

1 A woman is _____ someone on her phone.

2 A man is _____ to someone on his phone.

3 People are _____ while _____ at their phones.

4 A woman is _____ a picture with her camera.

5 A computer is _____ an ad on a website.

(▶) **3** **Watch again. Circle the correct answers.**

1 The amount of data is growing by 2.5 *million* / *billion* gigabytes every day.

2 All that data is worth a lot of *money* / *time*.

3 Mike Baker decided to help change the world of *traveling* / *advertising*.

4 Companies could predict what people might want to *buy* / *sell*.

5 Personalized ads are sent to *companies* / *customers*.

4 UNDERSTANDING MAIN IDEAS **Match the sentence halves.**

1 The amount of data is growing because _____

2 Using data is difficult because _____

3 Mike Baker found a partner because _____

4 You can't get away from ads completely because _____

5 Mike hunts data because _____

a he needed help.

b there is too much of it.

c we leave information every time we call, text, or search online.

d it is worth a lot of money.

e we live in a world of personalized ads.

💡 CRITICAL THINKING

5 **Work in small groups. Discuss the questions.**

ANALYZE

What are some differences between ads on TV, in newspapers or magazines, and online?

ANALYZE

What kinds of ads do you prefer to see on your phone or computer?

CREATE

Create an ad for your favorite product.

🐾 COLLABORATION

6 Debate: *Should companies be able to collect and use your personal information when you visit their websites or use their apps?*

A Work in small groups. Choose one side in the debate. Prepare your arguments. Think of at least three reasons to support your side.

B Find a group with the opposite opinion. Have an informal debate in front of the class. Then the class decides the debate winners.

WEATHER AND CLIMATE

LEARNING OBJECTIVES

Key Reading Skills	Reading for details; using your knowledge to predict content
Additional Reading Skills	Understanding key vocabulary; reading for main ideas; recognizing text type; synthesizing
Language Development	Collocations with *temperature*; describing a graph

ACTIVATE YOUR KNOWLEDGE

1 Match the types of weather to the photos.

2 What is your favorite type of weather? Why?

3 What is your least favorite type of weather? Why?

4 Look at the large photo. What type of weather do you see?

snowy   sunny   rainy   windy

READING 1

1 UNDERSTANDING KEY VOCABULARY **You are going to read a text about extreme weather. Before you read, look at the definitions. Complete the sentences with the correct form of the words in bold.**

> **almost** (adv) not everything, but very close to it
>
> **cover** (v) to lie on the surface of something
>
> **dangerous** (adj) can harm or hurt someone or something
>
> **huge** (adj) extremely large in size or amount
>
> **last** (v) to continue for a period of time
>
> **lightning** (n) a flash of bright light in the sky during a storm
>
> **thunder** (n) the sudden loud noise that comes after a flash of lightning

1 I think the big snow storm will _____ the ground in snow.
   We won't be able to see any grass at all.

2 Although _____ can be very scary, it is also beautiful when it
   flashes in the sky.

3 _____ every house on our street was destroyed by the fire.
   Only two houses were saved.

4   Asli got sick when the weather changed. Luckily, it didn't _____
    long. She felt better after a couple of days.

5   The _____ scared our cats. They wouldn't come out from under
    the bed until the storm ended and it was quiet again.

6   There has been a _____ increase in rainfall this year. As a result,
    the lakes and rivers are at the highest levels in years.

7   Swimming in the rain can be fun, but it's _____ if there is
    lightning. You should get out of the water right away so you don't
    get hurt.

2 USING YOUR KNOWLEDGE   **Work with a partner and discuss the questions.**

1   What kind of weather do you have in your town or city?
2   What does the word *extreme* mean?
3   What is an example of extreme weather?

EXTREME WEATHER

1 Extreme weather is when the weather is very different from normal. Extreme weather can take place over an hour, a day, or a long period of time. It can be **dangerous**, and in some cases, it can cause natural disasters[1].

Hurricanes

2 A hurricane is a type of storm. These storms are also called cyclones or typhoons. In North America and Central America, they are called hurricanes; in the North Pacific, they are called typhoons; and in the Indian Ocean and South Pacific, they are called cyclones. These storms are **huge**—they can be over 300 miles (500 kilometers) wide. They start over the ocean and move toward land. When they come to land, they bring **thunder**, **lightning**, strong winds, and very heavy rain. They can be very dangerous and destroy buildings, and even kill people.

Heat waves and droughts

3 A heat wave is when there are high temperatures and it is much hotter than normal. In many areas, heat waves are not a problem. However, in parts of the U.S., temperatures may reach above 120°F (49°C) in a heat wave, and **last** for a few days or several months. And in some places such as California, heat waves can cause droughts[2]. In a drought, there is not enough water for farmers to grow food. In some cases, people die because they don't have enough water to drink. Droughts are common in many countries in Africa, but in the last ten years, droughts also happened in Afghanistan, China, and Iran.

Rainstorms

4 Too much rain can cause floods[3]. Floods can destroy buildings and kill people. They can also destroy plants and food, which can mean that there is not enough food for people to eat. In 2015, there were very bad floods in South America. In Argentina, the Paraguay River was **almost** 50 feet (15 meters) higher than normal, and water **covered** the streets. In Paraguay, hundreds of thousands of people had to leave their homes. Strong winds damaged the power lines, and several people died. It was the worst flood in 50 years.

Sandstorms

5 A sandstorm is a large storm of dust and sand with strong winds. Sandstorms can be very dangerous. It is difficult to travel by car because people can't see anything. Even walking can be difficult. Sandstorms are common in the Middle East and in China. One of the worst sandstorms was in Iraq in 2011 when a storm lasted a whole week, causing many people to have breathing problems.

[1]**disaster** (n) an event that causes a lot of harm or damage

[2]**drought** (n) a long period when there is no rain and people do not have enough water

[3]**flood** (n) if a place floods or is flooded, it becomes covered in water

3 READING FOR MAIN IDEAS **Read the text on pages 72–73. Then circle the statement that contains the most important idea in each paragraph.**

1 Paragraph 1

   a Extreme weather is unusual and can cause natural disasters.
   b Extreme weather can take place over a short time or a long time.

2 Paragraph 2

   a Hurricanes cover a very wide area.
   b Hurricanes are huge, dangerous storms.

3 Paragraph 3

   a In a heat wave, temperatures are hotter than normal.
   b Heat waves sometimes occur in the U.S.

4 Paragraph 4

   a In 2015, there were floods in South America.
   b Floods happen when there is too much rain.

5 Paragraph 5

   a A sandstorm is a storm with a lot of wind and dust.
   b Certain countries have frequent sandstorms.

SKILLS

READING FOR DETAILS

When reading a text, it is important to understand the details as well as the main ideas. Details give specific information about the main ideas. You can find details in a text by looking for key words. Read the sentences with the key words carefully to understand important information.

 4 READING FOR DETAILS **Circle the correct ending for each sentence.**

1 Hurricanes move from …

   a land to sea.
   b sea to land.

2 Heat waves …

   a may lead to droughts.
   b aren't usually a big problem.

3 Paraguay had …

   a a very big flood in 2015.
   b no food for people to eat in 2015.

4 In 2011, …

   a China had a bad sandstorm.
   b Iraq had a bad sandstorm.

READING BETWEEN THE LINES

5 RECOGNIZING TEXT TYPE   **Circle the correct answer.**

1   What type of text is this?

    a an excerpt from a newspaper   **b** an excerpt from a textbook

2   Who would be interested in reading this text?

    a someone studying biology   **b** someone studying climate

3   What kind of information is included in the text?

    a facts   **b** opinions

⚙ CRITICAL THINKING

6 **Discuss the questions with a partner.**

APPLY	ANALYZE	EVALUATE
Do you prefer hot or cold weather?	What is the worst weather you have experienced? Describe it.	Has the weather in your country changed in recent years? Why or why not?

🗣 COLLABORATION

7 **A** Work in a small group. Choose a natural disaster, such as a flood, hurricane, or earthquake, that happened in your state or country. Go online and find the following information.

• What kind of natural disaster was it?

• Where did it happen?

• When did it happen?

• What happened?

• What did people do to help?

• Will it probably happen again?

    B Give a report to the class. Include photos or videos in your report.

READING 2

 1 UNDERSTANDING KEY VOCABULARY **Read the sentences. Write the words in bold next to the definitions.**

1 It was hot and sunny all day, so it was a **shock** when it suddenly started to rain.

2 The temperature will **rise** over the summer months. It will get hotter every day.

3 Let's wait and see what the weather is like tomorrow. Then we'll **decide** if we want to go to the beach or to a museum.

4 Be **careful** when you drive on icy roads. Go slowly and watch out for other cars.

5 Lloró, Colombia has the most **precipitation** in the world. It gets about 41.6 feet (12.7 meters) of rain every year.

6 The temperature might **drop**, so we'll build a fire to stay warm.

a _____ (adj) paying attention to what you are doing so that you do not have an accident, make a mistake, or damage something

b _____ (v) to decrease; to fall or go down

c _____ (v) to choose between one possibility or another

d _____ (n) a big, unpleasant surprise

e _____ (v) to increase; to go up

f _____ (n) rain or snow that falls to the ground

🔧 SKILLS

USING YOUR KNOWLEDGE TO PREDICT CONTENT

You can understand something better if you connect it to what you already know. Before you read something, first think about what you already know about the topic. This gets you ready for reading and helps you understand.

2 USING YOUR KNOWLEDGE **You are going to read about the Sahara Desert. Before you read, try to answer the questions.**

1   Where is the Sahara Desert?

   a   South Africa

   b   North Africa

   c   Central Africa

2   What is the weather like there?

   a   hot and dry

   b   cold and wet

   c   hot and wet

3 After you read the article on pages 78–79, check your answers to Exercise 2.

SURVIVING[1] THE SEA OF SAND

HOW TO STAY ALIVE IN THE SAHARA DESERT

BRAD ROGERS

1 Can you imagine a sea of sand three times bigger than India? This is the Sahara Desert, the largest desert in the world. It covers 11 countries in North Africa and is over 3 million square miles (9 million square kilometers). That's more than 25% of Africa.

2 In the Sahara, temperatures are very different during the day and at night. It is much hotter during the day than at night. During the day, the hottest time is between 2 p.m. and 4 p.m., when temperatures **rise** to 91°F (33°C). But it is very cold at night—the coldest time is at 4 a.m., when temperatures fall to 30°F (-1°C). The Sahara is very dry. The average **precipitation** in a year is only 3 inches (70 millimeters).

3 Because of the extreme temperatures in the desert, it is a very difficult place to survive. Marco Rivera, our survival expert, has some tips.

4 Take warm clothes and a blanket. You will need a hat, long pants, and a wool sweater to keep you warm at night. During the day, cover your body, head, and face. Clothes protect you from the sun and keep water in your body. You will also need a warm blanket at night. It can get cold very quickly. When the temperature **drops**, it can be a **shock** and make you feel even colder.

5 A car is easier to see than a person walking in the desert. You can also use the mirrors from your car to signal[2] to planes and other cars. You can use your car tires to make a fire. A fire is easy to see. It will help people find you, and it will keep you warm at night.

6 Try to drink some water at least once every hour. You need your water to last as long as possible. Drink only what you need. When you talk, you lose water from your body. Keep your mouth closed and do not talk.

7 If you eat, you will get thirsty and drink all of your water more quickly. You can eat a little, but only to stop you from feeling very hungry. Eat very small amounts of food, and eat very slowly. You can live three weeks with no food, but you can only live three days with no water.

8 It is very important to stay out of the sun during the day. Make a hole under your car and lie there. This will keep you cool and help you sleep. Find a warm place to sleep at night. A small place near a tree or a rock will be the warmest. But be **careful** before you **decide** where to sleep. Dangerous animals like snakes and scorpions also like to sleep in these places. Look carefully for animals before you lie down.

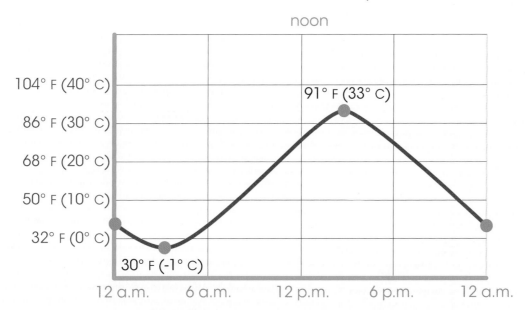

¹**surviving** (v) staying alive in dangerous situations

²**signal** (v) make a sign or wave to get someone's attention

4 READING FOR MAIN IDEAS **Read the article on pages 78–79. Write the paragraph numbers next to the best headings for the expert's tips.**

a Stay out of the Sun _____

b Drink Water _____

c Stay Cool During the Day and Warm at Night _____

d Don't Eat Too Much _____

e Stay with Your Car _____

5 READING FOR DETAILS **Match the sentence halves. Use the graph and information in paragraph 2 of Reading 2 to help you.**

1 The coldest time is

2 The average amount of rain in a year

3 The temperature is 91°F (33°C)

4 The coldest temperature at night

a between 2 p.m. and 4 p.m.

b is 30°F (-1°C).

c is 3 inches (70 mm).

d at four o'clock in the morning.

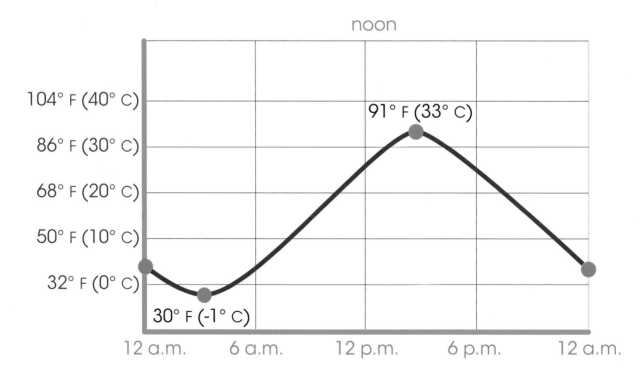

READING BETWEEN THE LINES

6 RECOGNIZING TEXT TYPE **Where might you find an article like this?**

a   in a newspaper

b   in a travel magazine

c   in a math textbook

⚙ CRITICAL THINKING

7 SYNTHESIZING **Work with a partner. Read the list of items. Use ideas from Reading 1 and Reading 2 to discuss the questions.**

- a blanket
- a mirror
- five gallons of water

- a radio
- a map
- a cell phone

- a hat
- boots
- a lighter

APPLY

Imagine you are alone in the desert. What three things do you need the most?

APPLY

Think of a different place. What three things do you need the most there?

EVALUATE

Compare your answers with your partner. Explain your reasons.

🖧 COLLABORATION

8 **A**   Work in a small group. Make a survival guide for each extreme weather situation in Reading 1. Write at least five survival tips for each situation.

B   Present your survival guides to the class. Your survival guides can be presentations, posters, or pamphlets.

COLLOCATIONS WITH *TEMPERATURE*

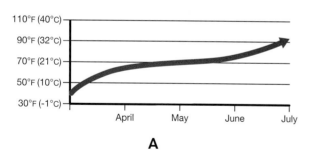

A

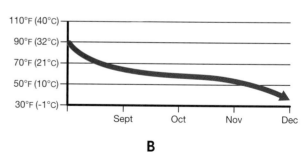

B

1 Look at the graphs. Circle the correct word to complete the sentences about the graphs.

1 In July, there are *high / low* temperatures.

2 In December, there are *high / low* temperatures.

3 The *maximum / minimum* temperature is 90°F (32°C) in July.

4 The *maximum / minimum* temperature is 34°F (1°C) in December.

DESCRIBING A GRAPH

LANGUAGE

You can use certain words and phrases to talk about graphs. Use the verbs *rise, drop, fall,* and *reach* and the nouns *increase* and *decrease* to describe changes on a graph. *Increase* and *decrease* are also verbs.

2 Match the sentences to the correct graph (A or B).

1 The graph shows an **increase** in temperature. _____

2 The graph shows a **decrease** in temperature. _____

3 The temperature **rises** to 90°F (32°C). _____

4 The temperature **drops** to 34°F (1°C). _____

5 The temperature **falls** to 34°F (1°C). _____

6 The temperature **reaches** 90°F (32°C). _____

3 Complete the statements with the bold words in Exercise 2.

1   Use _____ and _____ to talk about an *increase* in temperature.

2   Use _____ and _____ to talk about a *decrease* in temperature.

4 Look at the graphs. Circle the correct word to complete the sentences.

1
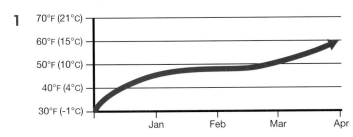

a   The graph shows *an increase / a decrease* in temperature.

b   In April, the temperature *reaches / falls* to 60°F (15°C).

2
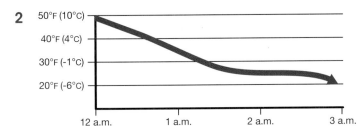

a   The graph shows *an increase / a decrease* in temperature.

b   At three o'clock, the temperature *drops / rises* to about 23°F (-5°C).

3
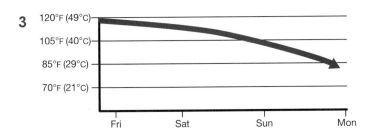

a   The graph shows *an increase / a decrease* in temperature.

b   On Monday, the temperature *reaches / falls to* 86°F (30°C).

4
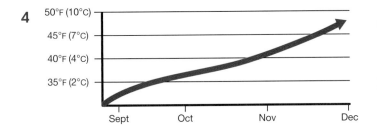

a   The graph shows *an increase / a decrease* in temperature.

b   In December, the temperature *rises / falls* to 45°F (7°C).

WATCH AND LISTEN

PREPARING TO WATCH

1 ACTIVATING YOUR KNOWLEDGE **Work with a partner and answer the questions.**

1 What is a thunderstorm?
2 Why are some people afraid of thunderstorms?
3 How can wind from a storm be dangerous?

2 PREDICTING CONTENT USING VISUALS **Look at the pictures from the video. Discuss the questions with your partner.**

1 What do you think the video is about?
2 Where do you think it takes place?
3 What do you think the man's job is?

WHILE WATCHING

3 UNDERSTANDING DETAILS **Watch the video. Circle the correct answers.**

1 The middle of the United States is called Tornado *Alley* / *Valley*.
2 The year *2010* / *2011* was very bad for tornadoes.
3 That year a dangerous tornado killed more than *160* / *60* people.
4 Scientists *can* / *cannot* predict when and where tornadoes will happen.
5 Josh Wurman is a *computer* / *weather* scientist.
6 *Seventy-five* / *twenty-five* percent of thunderstorms produce tornadoes.
7 Finding the right thunderstorm is *easy* / *difficult*.

▶ **4** UNDERSTANDING DETAILS **Watch again. Match the questions to the correct answers.**

1 What does spring bring?

2 What killed people in Joplin, Missouri?

3 What is Josh Wurman studying?

4 What does Josh use to find storms?

5 Why did the team have to move fast?

a tornadoes

b warm, wet air

c a dangerous tornado

d tornadoes happen quickly

e a Doppler radar scanner

5 UNDERSTANDING MAIN IDEAS **Read the statements. What is the video mainly about? Circle the best answer.**

a Some thunderstorms produce tornadoes, but others do not.

b Tornadoes are one of the most dangerous kinds of weather in the world.

c The winds in a tornado can spin faster than the winds in a hurricane.

6 MAKING INFERENCES **Work with a partner. Do Josh and his team enjoy their work? How do you know?**

💡 CRITICAL THINKING

7 Work with a partner. Discuss the questions.

UNDERSTAND	ANALYZE	EVALUATE
Is Josh Wurman's job important? Why or why not?	What other jobs are related to weather?	Why do people choose to live in areas with extreme weather?

🗫 COLLABORATION

8 A Work with a partner. Interview a person who has been in a natural disaster. Prepare 5–10 questions.

B Interview the person. Take notes.

C Write a summary of the results, and share it with the class.

SPORTS AND COMPETITION

LEARNING OBJECTIVES

Key Reading Skill	Scanning to predict content
Additional Reading Skills	Understanding key vocabulary; reading for main ideas, reading for details; recognizing text type; previewing; predicting content using visuals; taking notes; understanding discourse; working out meaning; synthesizing
Language Development	Prepositions of movement

ACTIVATE YOUR KNOWLEDGE

Discuss the questions with a partner.

1. Look at the photo. What sport do you see?

2. Do you do or play any sports? Why or why not?

3. Do you like watching sports? If so, which sports do you enjoy watching?

4. Do you have a favorite team or sportsperson?

5. Why do you think people like watching sports?

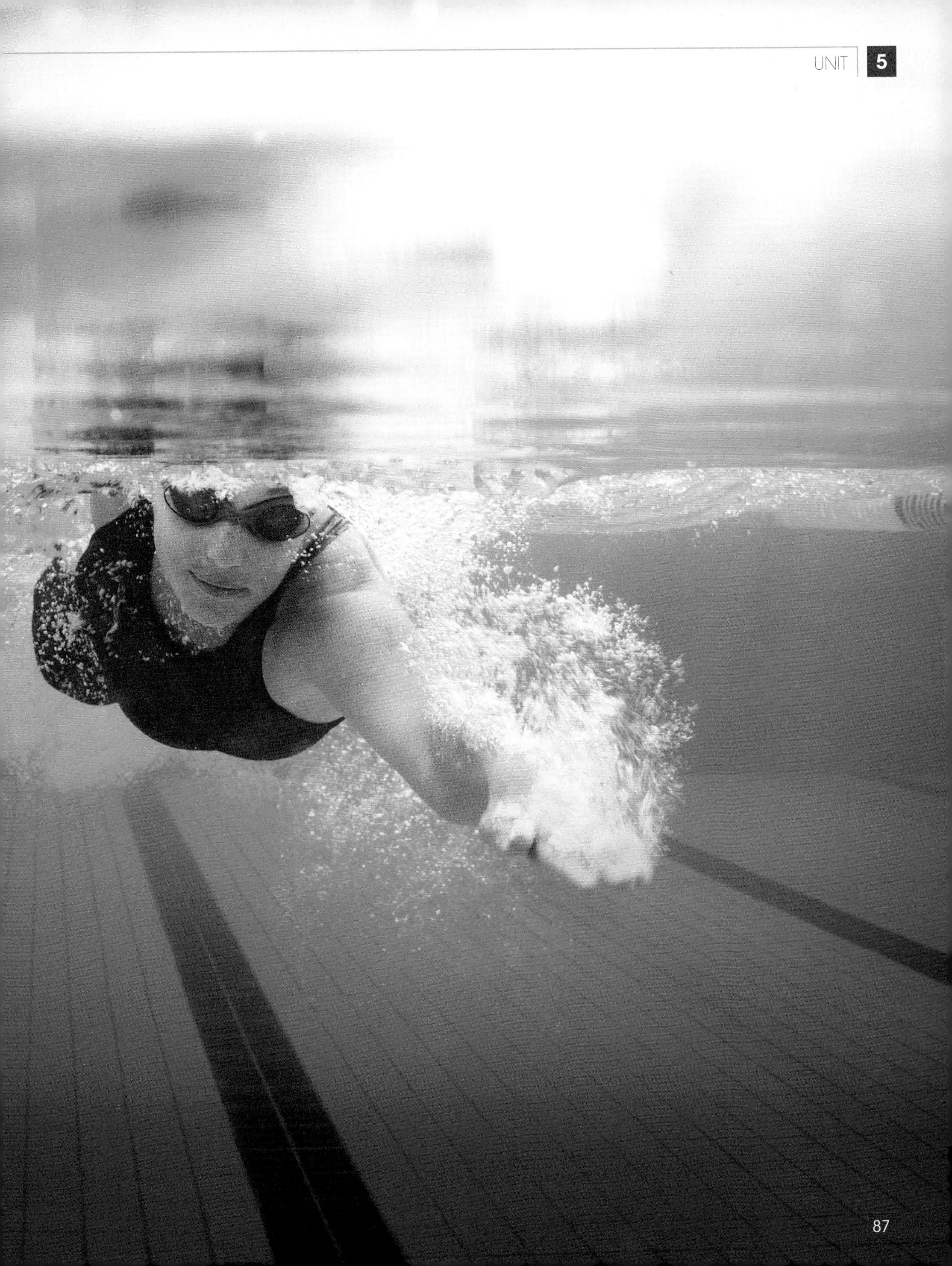

PREPARING TO READ

1 **UNDERSTANDING KEY VOCABULARY** **Read the definitions. Complete the sentences with the correct form of the words in bold.**

> **ancient** (adj) from a long time ago; very old
>
> **compete** (v) to take part in a race or competition; to try to be more successful than someone else
>
> **competition** (n) an organized event in which people try to win a prize by being the best
>
> **strange** (adj) not familiar; difficult to understand; different
>
> **swimming** (n) a sport where people move through water by moving their body
>
> **take place** (phr v) to happen
>
> **throw** (v) to send something through the air, pushing it out of your hand

1 The baseball game will _____ tomorrow at 2 p.m. in the park.

2 Thousands of people from all over the world _____ in the New York City Marathon every year. The fastest runners can win a lot of money.

3 Boxing is a(n) _____ sport; it was popular in Rome thousands of years ago.

4 The first cricket game I ever saw was _____ because I didn't understand the rules. Once I learned more about the sport, I became a big fan.

5 In baseball, players must be able to _____ the ball a long distance directly to another player.

6 The best tennis players were selected from each high school in the city. They will play in a(n) _____ to see who is the best tennis player in the city.

7 Because Elsa grew up near the ocean, her favorite sport was _____. Her parents said she was just like a fish.

🛠 SKILLS

SCANNING TO PREDICT CONTENT

Before reading a text, skilled readers often scan for *key words*. Key words are usually nouns, verbs, and adjectives. The key words tell the reader what the text is going to be about.

---

2 SCANNING TO PREDICT CONTENT **Look at the underlined words in paragraph 1 of the text on pages 90–91. Answer the questions.**

1 What is the main topic of the text?

   a unusual competitions

   b unusual sports

   c popular sports

2 Where do the events in the text happen?

   a in one country

   b around the world

   c in a city

3 Look at the underlined words again. What types of words are they? More than one answer is possible.

   a verbs

   b adjectives

   c articles

   d nouns

   e prepositions

3 **After you read the text, check your answers to Exercise 2.**

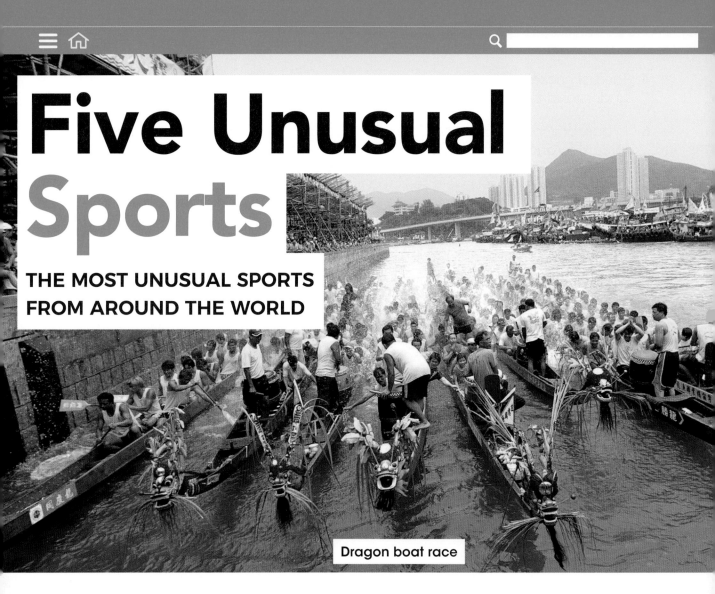

Five Unusual Sports

THE MOST UNUSUAL SPORTS FROM AROUND THE WORLD

Dragon boat race

1 Every <u>country</u> has a national <u>sport</u>, and most popular <u>sports</u> are now played across the <u>world</u>. Most people have heard of <u>sports</u> like football, basketball, baseball, and soccer. However, in most <u>countries</u>, people also play <u>unusual sports</u> with **strange** and interesting rules. Here are our top five <u>unusual sports</u> from around the world.

2 People go **swimming** in the Atlantic Ocean in the winter. They go swimming at the beach on Coney Island in New York City every Sunday from October to April and also on New Year's Day. The water temperature can drop to as low as 32° F (0° C). Sometimes there is snow and cold wind, too. People believe that swimming in the cold water is good for their health. The club started in 1903.

3 Every year in Singapore, thousands of people come to watch the dragon boat race. A dragon boat is a traditional Chinese boat with a painted dragon's head on one end. There are 22 people in each boat, and they race in the water. Dragon boat racing is also popular in China, Malaysia, and Indonesia.

4 In this sport, people **compete** by **throwing** a large piece of wood called a "caber" as far as they can. The caber toss is an **ancient** Scottish sport. The caber has no official size or shape, but it is usually the size of a small tree.

5 Students in Indonesia play this game to welcome the month of Ramadan. It is similar to soccer. The ball is made from coconut shells. Before starting the game, players pour salt on themselves and then light the ball on fire. The ball is on fire throughout the game, and the players play with their bare[1] feet.

6 In Turkey, camel wrestling[2] is a very old sport. The largest camel wrestling **competition takes place** in Ephesus every year, and thousands of people come to watch. In the sport, two male camels wrestle each other. Sometimes the camels do not want to fight, and they run through the crowds, which can be dangerous.

[1]**bare** (adj) without shoes

[2]**wrestling** (n) a sport in which two people (or, in this case, animals) fight and try to push each other to the ground

Caber toss

WHILE READING

4 READING FOR MAIN IDEAS **Read the text on pages 90–91. Write the correct heading above each paragraph in the text.**

a Fireball Soccer

b Dragon Boat Racing

c Camel Wrestling

d Caber Toss

e Coney Island Polar Bear Plunge

5 **Write the names of the countries where each sport is popular.**

1 Fireball soccer _____

2 Dragon boat race _____

3 Camel wrestling _____

4 Caber toss _____

5 Coney Island Polar Bear Plunge _____

Polar Bear Plunge

 6 READING FOR DETAILS **Read the text again and look at the sentences. There is one mistake in each sentence. Correct the false information.**

1 The Coney Island Polar Bear Plunge takes place on Christmas Day.

2 The Coney Island Polar Bear Plunge began in 2003.

3 A dragon boat has a dragon's tail painted on it.

4 There are 25 people in each dragon boat team.

5 A caber is a large piece of metal.

6 A caber is usually the size of a large tree.

7 In fireball soccer, the ball is made from plastic.

8 The ball is on fire only at the beginning of a game of fireball soccer.

9   The Ephesus camel wrestling competition happens twice a year.

10 In camel wrestling, two female camels fight each other

READING BETWEEN THE LINES

7 RECOGNIZING TEXT TYPE **Answer the questions.**

1   What kind of person is this text for?

   a someone who is interested in different sports

   b someone who wants to learn how to play a
      new sport

2   Where do you think you might see this text?

   a in a newspaper or magazine

   b on a website

3   What do you think the text is?

   a an advertisement

   b an article

Camel Wrestling

·☼· CRITICAL THINKING

8 **Discuss the questions with a partner.**

ANALYZE	**ANALYZE**	**EVALUATE**
What are the advantages of playing sports?	Why do countries spend money on sports like the Olympics?	Compare three sports in Reading 1. How are they similar? How are they different?

⚙ COLLABORATION

9 **A** Work in a small group. Choose an unusual sport or competition. Imagine that you must convince your school to start a team. Think of at least five reasons to support your sport.

   B Describe the sport and present your reasons to the class. As a class, vote for the winner.

READING 2

1 UNDERSTANDING KEY VOCABULARY **Read the sentences and choose the best definition for the words in bold.**

1 In January 2015, the Hong Kong Marathon had over 73,000 **participants**.

   a people who take part in an activity

   b people who organize an activity

2 The golf **course** was so big that the players drove golf carts to get from hole to hole.

   a an area used for sporting events, such as racing or playing golf

   b an area where players get together after they finish a sport

3 It takes about six hours to **climb** Mount Fuji in Japan. Many people try to reach the top just before the sun rises.

   a wait for something to start

   b go up something or onto the top of something

4 There was an **accident** during the car race yesterday. One car hit another, and they both rolled over. Luckily, neither driver was hurt.

   a something bad that happens that is not intended and that causes injury or damage

   b something that someone does in order to hurt another person

Climbing Mt. Fuji

5   In order to stay **in shape**, you should eat foods that are good for you, exercise, and stay active.

    a interesting because you like different things

    b in good health; strong

6   One of the most **challenging** games is table tennis, which is also called Ping-Pong. Players must be strong, quick, and able to focus on the ball for long periods of time.

    a easy to learn

    b difficult in a way that tests your ability

2 PREVIEWING **Before you read, look at the text on pages 96–97. What type of text is it? How do you know?**

1   type of text _____

2   reasons for my answer: _____

_____

3 PREDICTING CONTENT USING VISUALS **Look at the photos and read the title of the text. What do you think the topic of the text will be? How do you know?**

1   topic of text _____

2   reasons for my answer: _____

_____

4 **After you read the text, check your answers to Exercises 2 and 3.**

TOUGH GUY:
A RACE TO THE LIMIT

1 **What is Tough[1] Guy?**

Every January, more than 3,000 people take part in one of the most difficult races on Earth: the Tough Guy competition in the United Kingdom. **Participants** run, swim, and **climb** across the 9-mile (15-kilometer) **course**. But this is no normal race. These runners have to crawl through tunnels, run across a field of nettles, and jump over fire. What's more, the competition takes place in January, so temperatures are freezing—sometimes as low as 21° F (-6° C). People travel from all over the world to take part, with participants from the United States, Australia, and China.

2 Why do people take part?

The competition is very dangerous and every year there are **accidents**. Injuries like broken bones and cuts are common. The race is very hard: one-third of participants do not finish it. Runners have to be healthy and **in shape**. Most people train all year to prepare for the event. It is also the first race like it in the world. Many people take part in the competition because it is so famous. Every year, the organizers change the event and add new things. This means that the competition stays exciting and **challenging**, so people go back year after year.

3 The course

The diagram shows an example of the Tough Guy course. First, participants run for 0.6 miles (1 kilometer) along a muddy road. Next, they crawl under low nets on the ground. After the nets, the runners jump off a high platform into a lake and swim for another 0.6 miles (1 kilometer). Then they reach the field of fire. Here the runners run across a field and jump over small bonfires. Next, participants must crawl through a long tunnel. The tunnel is partly underwater. Finally, the runners run 1.2 miles (2 kilometers) through nettles before they reach the finish line.

" The race is very hard: one-third of participants do not finish it.

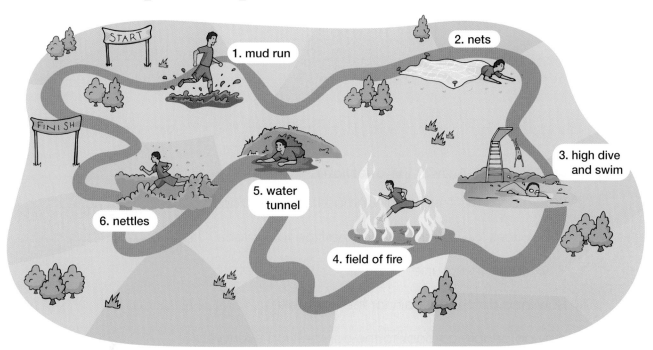

1. mud run
2. nets
3. high dive and swim
4. field of fire
5. water tunnel
6. nettles

¹tough (adj) physically strong and not afraid

5 READING FOR MAIN IDEAS **Read the text on pages 96–97. Circle the correct words to complete the sentences.**

1 Tough Guy is a very *easy* / *difficult* competition.
2 The event takes place when it is very *hot* / *cold*.
3 People from many different *countries* / *cities* take part.
4 Every year, people get *hurt* / *leave early*.
5 Participants have to be very *smart* / *strong* to do the event.
6 The competition is *different* / *the same* every year.

6 TAKING NOTES **Look at the diagram and part 3 on page 97. Complete the student's notes with the correct sections of the course.**

section of course	description of section
(1)	crawl through something wet
(2)	run & jump over small bonfires
(3)	run 1.2 miles through dangerous plants
(4)	run 0.6 miles along wet & dirty road
(5)	jump off platform into lake
(6)	crawl low on ground

7 READING FOR DETAILS **Answer the questions.**

1 Where does the Tough Guy competition take place? _____

2 When does the Tough Guy competition take place? _____

3 How long is the course? _____

4 How long do people train for the competition? _____

5 Why do people go back to the competition every year?

_____

8 UNDERSTANDING DISCOURSE **Match the verbs to the correct phrases. Each verb has two answers.**

1 crawl _____ _____

2 run _____ _____

3 jump _____ _____

a over small bonfires

b across a field of nettles

c under low nets

d across a field of fire

e through tunnels

f off a high platform

READING BETWEEN THE LINES

9 WORKING OUT MEANING **Circle the correct answer.**

1 The text says that participants have to *run through nettles*. Read the text again. What is a nettle?

a a plant

b an animal

2 Why do you think running through nettles is difficult?

a because nettles hurt you

b because nettles smell horrible

☼ CRITICAL THINKING

10 SYNTHESIZING **Work with a partner. Use ideas from Reading 1 and Reading 2 to discuss the questions.**

APPLY

Do you know any events like the Tough Guy competition?

ANALYZE

Why do people stay in shape in their free time?

EVALUATE

Should people be allowed to do dangerous sports?

🤝 COLLABORATION

11 **A** Work with a partner. Write 5–10 interview questions to ask a Tough Guy participant.

B Role-play an interview. One of you is the sports reporter and one of you is the Tough Guy participant.

LANGUAGE DEVELOPMENT

PREPOSITIONS OF MOVEMENT

> **LANGUAGE**
>
> *Prepositions of movement* describe where someone or something is going. Use prepositions of movement to give directions.
>
> Walk **past** the school and **across** the road.

1 Match the descriptions to the pictures.

1 past the building ———

2 through the tunnel ———

3 across the lake ———

4 around the track ———

5 along the road ———

6 over the bridge ———

7 under the bridge ———

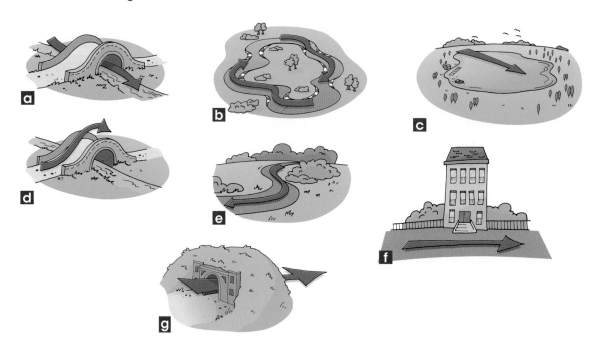

2 Underline the prepositions of movement in Exercise 1.

3 Look at the map. Use the prepositions from Exercise 1 to complete the paragraph. You may need to use some prepositions more than once.

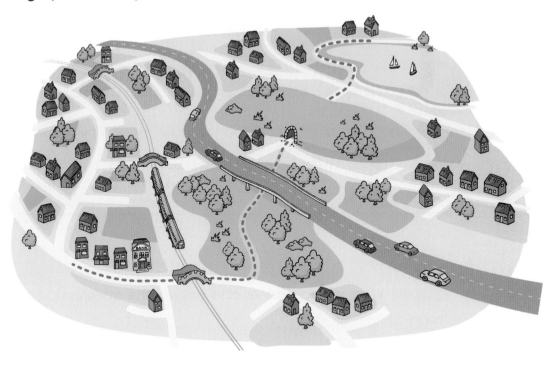

It is easy to get to my house. First, walk (1) _____ Main Street. Go (2) _____ the bank and (3) _____ the bridge. Then walk (4) _____ the park and (5) _____ the next bridge. Go (6) _____ the tunnel—watch out for cars— and walk (7) _____ the road. Walk (8) _____ the lake. My house is at the end of the road.

4 Give directions from your home to school or work. Write at least five sentences. Use prepositions of movement.

_____

_____

_____

_____

_____

WATCH AND LISTEN

GLOSSARY

slalom (n) a race, especially down a mountain on skis, in which the competitors follow a path that curves around a series of poles

smooth (adj) having a surface with no holes or lumps in it; glass is usually smooth

wax (n) a solid substance that becomes soft when warm and melts easily, often used to make candles

PREPARING TO WATCH

1 ACTIVATING YOUR KNOWLEDGE **Work with a partner and answer the questions.**

1 What are some mountain sports?

2 What sports include racing?

3 What sports are in the Winter Olympics?

2 PREDICTING CONTENT USING VISUALS **You are going to watch a video about a winter sport. Look at the pictures from the video. What are the people doing? Discuss your answers with your partner.**

WHILE WATCHING

3 UNDERSTANDING DETAILS **Watch the video. Complete each sentence with a word from the box. You will use five of the seven words.**

> best blue dangerous green
> popular rich well-known

1 Courchevel is a very _____ place for skiing.

2 Some of the world's _____ skiers go to Courchevel.

3 Courchevel 1850 is the highest and most _____ village.

4 Many _____ and famous people like to ski here.

5 Slalom skiers race down the mountain between _____ and red flags.

▶ **4** **Watch again. Correct the mistakes in the sentences.**

1 Emma is a British Olympic swimmer.

2 She was in the Olympics two times.

3 Dallas Campbell is an Olympic skier.

4 Emma and Dallas are racing up the mountain.

5 The difference between 1st and 10th place is less than one minute.

6 Wax makes skis go slow.

▶ **5** UNDERSTANDING MAIN IDEAS **Watch again. How do they prepare the skis? Put the steps in the order you hear them (1–4). Compare your answers with a partner.**

a Then they make the skis smooth again. _____

b Next, they fill the holes with wax. _____

c The skis are now ready. _____

d First, they grind the bottom of the skis. _____

6 MAKING INFERENCES **Work with a partner. What are two other reasons people might go to Courchevel?**

☀ CRITICAL THINKING

7 **Work with a partner. Discuss the questions.**

APPLY	APPLY	EVALUATE
Do you think skiing is easy? Is it dangerous? Explain your answers.	What are some racing sports in your country?	Have you ever been in a race? Would you recommend it?

COLLABORATION

8 **A** Work in a small group. Invent a new type of sport or competition. Think about:

- the name
- the equipment
- the number of players
- the rules

B Make a poster for your sport or competition. Include the rules, pictures or drawings, and any other important information. Present your poster to the class.

BUSINESS

LEARNING OBJECTIVES

Key Reading Skills	Working out meaning from context; annotating
Additional Reading Skills	Understanding key vocabulary; scanning to predict content; reading for main ideas; reading for details; giving opinions; identifying audience; making inferences; synthesizing
Language Development	Collocations with *business*; business vocabulary

ACTIVATE YOUR KNOWLEDGE

1 Discuss the questions with a partner.

An *entrepreneur* is a person who starts a new business. Do you know the names of the famous entrepreneurs in the small photos?

Do you know the names of the companies they started?

Do you know the names of any other famous entrepreneurs from your country?

2 Look at the words in the box. Which of these are important qualities for an entrepreneur to have?

> careful smart friendly good with computers polite good with money happy hardworking kind funny

3 Do you think you would be a good entrepreneur? Why or why not?

READING 1

1 UNDERSTANDING KEY VOCABULARY **Read the sentences and choose the best definition for the words in bold.**

1 Marta likes to **organize** her schedule at work. She puts her meetings and tasks in a calendar so that she gets everything done on time.

   a plan or arrange carefully

   b lose easily

2 Ken found a job he wants to do. He wants to **apply** for it this week and hopes to get the job.

   a share thoughts and ideas

   b ask officially for something, often by writing

3 Emre just shared the **results** of the company survey. He says that a lot of people are happy with the company's work.

   a information that you find out from something, such as an exam, a scientific experiment, or a medical test

   b questions people ask to find out more information

4 Grace is trying to decide on an **occupation**. She wants to be either a doctor or an engineer.

   a homework

   b a job or career

5 My **colleague** and I are writing a new computer program. We work late every night because our boss wants us to finish it quickly.

    a someone that you live next to

    b someone that you work with

6 The new store on Main Street is doing really well. A lot of **customers** go there and buy things.

    a people who buy things from a store or business

    b people who sell things at a store or business

2 SCANNING TO PREDICT CONTENT **Before you read, look at the text on pages 108–109 quickly. Circle the answers.**

1 What kind of text is it?

    a an encyclopedia entry

    b a quiz

    c a newspaper article

2 Which question is the best description of the topic?

    a What would be your perfect job?

    b Could you start your own company?

    c What makes a good businessperson?

3 **After you read the text, check your answers in Exercise 2.**

SURVEY ARE YOU READY FOR THE WORLD OF WORK?

Do you know what kind of job you want? Before you **apply** for a job, think about the different types of jobs that people do. There are four main types of jobs:

1 jobs with people

2 jobs with information

3 jobs with things

4 jobs with ideas

Check your **results** and read the advice to find **occupations** you would like.

What kind of work would be best for you? Take our quiz and find out about the kind of work you would enjoy. For each question, choose the best answer for you: **a, b, c, or d**.

1 What do you like to do in the evenings?

○ **a** meet friends or go to a party

○ **b** stay at home and surf the Internet

○ **c** play sports or practice a hobby like a musical instrument or photography

○ **d** go to the movies

2 Which sections of the newspaper do you look at first?

○ **a** advice column or letters to the editor

○ **b** news

○ **c** sports

○ **d** TV, music, books, and art

3 What do you like to do at a party?

○ **a** meet new people

○ **b** discuss the latest news

○ **c** help with the food and drinks

○ **d** sing songs and tell jokes

4 What do you prefer to do on a day off?

○ **a** have coffee with friends

○ **b** **organize** your books and cabinets

○ **c** work in the garden or clean your house

○ **d** write poetry, make music, or draw pictures

EXPLANATION OF RESULTS

Mostly "a" answers:

You are friendly, kind, and interested in other people. You would enjoy a job working with children, **customers** in a store, or on a team with **colleagues**. Possible jobs are: teacher, waiter, police officer.

Mostly "b" answers:

You are neat, good at planning, and you like learning new things. You would enjoy a job working with information. Possible jobs are: college professor, computer programmer, librarian.

Mostly "c" answers:

You are practical, good at sports, and you like working with your hands. You would enjoy a job working with things. Possible jobs are: construction worker, engineer, farmer.

Mostly "d" answers:

You are creative, good at music and art, and you like books. You would enjoy a job working with ideas. Possible jobs are: artist, writer, singer.

4 READING FOR MAIN IDEAS **Read the text on pages 108–109. Find and correct five mistakes in the paragraph below.**

> There are three main kinds of work – work with animals, work with information, work with machines, and work with ideas. The quiz helps you to find out about the kind of people you might like. After the quiz, read the advice to find universities you may like.

5 READING FOR DETAILS **Take the quiz. Circle your answers and count the letters you chose. Read the advice about jobs for you.**

6 GIVING OPINIONS **Do you agree or disagree with the advice? Why?**

READING BETWEEN THE LINES

7 WORKING OUT MEANING **Find the words from the box in the text and underline them.**

hobby	neat	advice	sections

8 **Read the text around the words you underlined in the text. Circle the best definition for each word.**

1 advice (n)
   a an opinion that someone offers you about what you should do
   b instructions to tell someone exactly what to do

2 hobby (n)
   a an activity you do for fun
   b a job

3 section (n)
   a a type of reading material
   b one of the parts that something is divided into

4 neat (adj)
   a arranged well, with everything in its place
   b not organized

9 IDENTIFYING AUDIENCE **Who would be interested in the quiz? Circle the correct answer. More than one answer is possible.**

   a a new worker in a company
   b a new college graduate
   c a high school student

☼ CRITICAL THINKING

10 **Discuss the questions with a partner.**

APPLY	EVALUATE	EVALUATE
Describe a job you did in the past.	What would be your perfect job? Why?	What type of job would you hate? Why?

🐾 COLLABORATION

11 **A** Work in a small group. Write 10 job interview questions.

   B Take turns interviewing for your dream job.

READING 2

1 UNDERSTANDING KEY VOCABULARY **Read the sentences and write the words in bold next to the definitions on page 113.**

1 I want to be a doctor. I can reach my **goal** by studying hard.

2 The company **introduced** a new tablet, and it sold out in one day.

3 A lot of new jobs were created by the automobile factory. They **employ** more than 300 people in the community.

4 Akiko shares an **office** with her coworker. It is small, and they don't have a lot of space for their desks and files.

5 Manuel is my business **partner**. We opened a restaurant together.

6 I'm going to **set up** a new business in my garage next year.

7 The company needs to **advertise** its new smartphone on TV and on the Internet so that more people know about it and want to buy it.

8 My mother **runs** her own business.

a _____ (phr v) to create or establish (something) for a particular purpose

b _____ (n) a place in a building where people work

c _____ (v) to manage or operate something

d _____ (n) someone who runs or owns a business with another person

e _____ (n) something you want to do successfully in the future

f _____ (v) to pay someone to work or do a job for you

g _____ (v) to make something available to buy or use for the first time

h _____ (v) to tell people about a product or service, for example in newspapers or on television, in order to persuade them to buy it

2 SCANNING TO PREDICT CONTENT **Look at the article on pages 114–115 and notice the words in bold from Exercise 1. Read the title.**

1 What do you think the article is about?

_____

2 What three words most helped you decide the topic of the article?

_____

_____

_____

THE STORY OF GOOGLE

Goals Then and Now

1 Google is a huge technology company. It specializes in online advertising and searching, as well as other Internet-related products. Google was started by Larry Page and Sergey Brin. They met at Stanford University in 1995. Their **goal** was to organize all of the information on the Web. Today, their company **employs** more than 40,000 people around the world. The two **partners** created a company that made searching the Internet easy. Now they focus on three main areas. They make sure their search engine[1] is fast and smart so that people can find information easily. They develop products that let people work on different devices and in different places. They help new businesses **advertise** and find new customers.

The Growth of Google

2   Google grew very quickly. Page and Brin registered[2] the domain name[3] Google. com in 1997. In 1998, they **set up** a small **office** in a garage and hired their first employee, Craig Silverstein. They **ran** their business in the garage until they could move to a larger space. In the busy years that followed, Google expanded its services. In 2000, people could do Internet searches in 15 languages, including Dutch, Chinese, and Korean. Today, people can search in more than 150,000 languages. Google **introduced** a map service in 2005 called Google Maps™. The same year, it came out with a program called Google Earth™. This program allowed users to see close-up pictures of cities and neighborhoods when they typed in an address. In 2006, the name "Google" became a verb in English dictionaries. This shows the company's influence on modern life.

Ideas and Creativity

3   Today, Google is a creative workplace where employees share ideas with each other. Page and Brin are available during the week to talk with their employees and answer questions. This open environment has resulted in many new ideas. In 2011, the company released a program called Google Art Project™ that helped people explore the world's top museums from their computer. As of 2018, Google was continuing its work on a self-driving car. In the future, this car could help people who can't see well to drive. The company extends its services to the community, too. In 2008, it started a yearly art contest for students. Every year, the winner's artwork appears on its homepage for one day. Google believes that creativity is important, both in the workplace and in the community. In addition to producing famous Internet products, Google gives people opportunities to be creative, which leads to success.

[1]**search engine** (n) a website used for finding specific information on the Internet

[2]**register** (v) put information on an official list

[3]**domain name** (n) the part of an email address or website address that shows the name of the organization that the address belongs to

✎ SKILLS

ANNOTATING

Effective readers take notes and *annotate* as they read. When you annotate, you write notes on the same page as the text. Annotating will help you remember key information. For example, you can underline, circle, or highlight important words, numbers, and ideas. You can write main ideas and definitions of words in the margin. Annotating a text can also help you to study for tests or write about a text. For example:

> *all the people able to work*
> A recent study showed that <u>10% of the American workforce</u> is made up of self-employed workers. The self-employed then provide jobs for an additional (29 million) people.

3 ANNOTATING **Read the article on pages 114–115, and annotate the important words, dates, numbers, and ideas. Compare your notes with a partner.**

4 READING FOR MAIN IDEAS **Read the questions and circle the correct answer.**

1 How does Google help new businesses?
a Google lets new businesses borrow money.
b Google helps new businesses find customers.

2 Where was Google's first office?
a in a garage
b at Stanford University

3 What does Google want its employees to do?
a share creative ideas with each other
b work at night and sometimes on weekends

4 Who might benefit from a self-driving car?
a people who have trouble seeing
b people who drive long distances to work

5 READING FOR DETAILS **Write *T* (true) or *F* (false) next to the statements. Then correct the false statements.**

_____ 1 Google's only focus is on making their search engine smart and fast.

_____ 2 In 2006, "Google" was added to dictionaries as a verb.

_____ 3 The original Google partners answer their employees' questions.

_____ 4 Google released a program that teaches people how to draw famous works of art.

READING BETWEEN THE LINES

6 MAKING INFERENCES **What do you think the creators of Google believe? Circle the answer.**

a Creativity is needed to be successful.

b Creativity is not important.

○ CRITICAL THINKING

7 SYNTHESIZING **Work with a partner. Use ideas from Reading 1 and Reading 2 to discuss the questions.**

ANALYZE	EVALUATE	CREATE
Why is Google so successful?	Would you like to have your own business? Why or why not?	If you had your own business, what would it be?

COLLABORATION

8 **A** Work in small groups. Think about your business idea in Exercise 7. How could you use Google products to help your business succeed? Research Google Ads, Google Analytics, and other Google products.

B Share what you learned with the class. Do other groups have ideas that would also work for your business?

COLLOCATIONS WITH *BUSINESS*

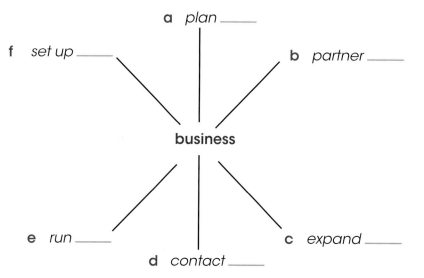

a *plan* _____

f *set up* _____

b *partner* _____

business

e *run* _____

c *expand* _____

d *contact* _____

1 The words in the diagram are collocations of *business*. Write **N** next to the nouns and **V** next to the verbs.

2 Use words from the diagram to complete the sentences.

1 *A business* _____ is a detailed document describing the future plans of a business.

2 _____ *a business* means to make a business bigger.

3 *A business* _____ is a person who owns a business with you.

4 _____ *a business* means to be in charge of and control a business.

5 _____ *a business* means to start a business.

6 *A business* _____ is a person you know because of your job.

3 Look at the sentences in Exercise 2 again and answer the questions.

1 Do the verbs go before or after the word *business*? _____

2 Do the nouns go before or after the word *business*? _____

BUSINESS VOCABULARY

4 **Match the words to their definitions.**

1 employ   a a type of computer program

2 employee   b to give someone a job

3 office   c a place where people work

4 software   d something a business makes to sell

5 product   e a worker

5 **Use the words from Exercise 4 to complete the email. You may need to use the plural form of some words.**

To	Whole Company
From	James Curry
Subject	Important information

Important information for all (1)_____ of Jenson Co. I am pleased
to tell you that we are moving into a bright new (2)_____ in three
months. We are also getting new (3)_____ for our computers. We
will have more space, so we can (4)_____ more people. I am
very confident that these changes will help us sell more of our excellent
(5)_____.

Best,
James Curry

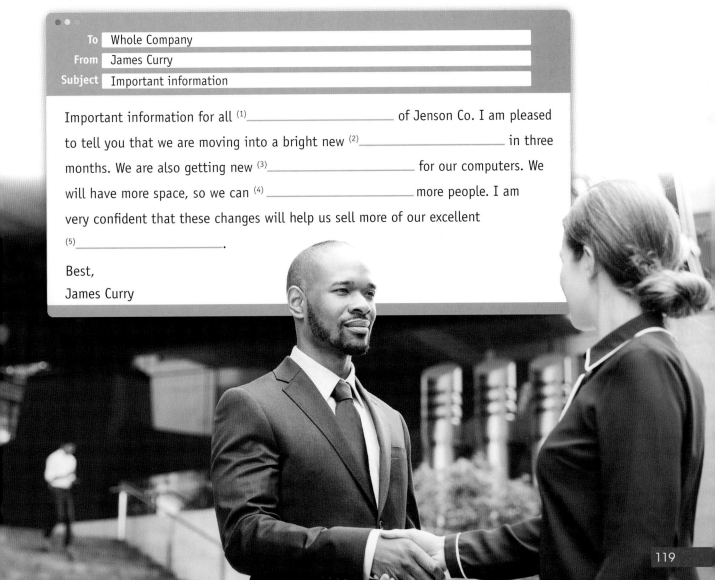

WATCH AND LISTEN

GLOSSARY

warehouse (n) a large building for keeping things that are going to be sold
item (n) a single thing in a set or on a list, such as a book or a toy
fulfillment (n) the act of doing something that you promised to do
central (adj) main or most important; organized and working from one main place
random (adj) done or chosen without any plan or system

PREPARING TO WATCH

1 ACTIVATING YOUR KNOWLEDGE **Work with a partner and answer the questions.**

1 Why do people shop online?
2 What do people usually buy online?
3 What was the last thing you bought online? What about in a store?

2 USING YOUR KNOWLEDGE **You are going to watch a video about the online store Amazon. Read the statements. Check (✓) the ones that you think are true.**

1 ☐ There are millions of things to buy at Amazon.
2 ☐ A computer finds your things after you order them.
3 ☐ Amazon does not sell kitchen things.

WHILE WATCHING

▶ **3** UNDERSTANDING DETAILS **Watch the video. Check your answers in Exercise 2.**

▶ **4** **Watch again. Put a check (✓) next to the things you see.**

1 ☐ a shelf
2 ☐ a green bin
3 ☐ a warehouse
4 ☐ a book
5 ☐ a truck

6 ☐ a male worker
7 ☐ a toy
8 ☐ a cell phone
9 ☐ a box
10 ☐ scissors

5 UNDERSTANDING MAIN IDEAS **Write *T* (true) or *F* (false) next to the statements. Correct the false statements.**

_____ 1 Amazon is the world's largest online store.

_____ 2 The first warehouse was a kitchen.

_____ 3 Only the workers know where everything is.

_____ 4 An Amazon worker finds your item before you pay for it.

_____ 5 Any item can be on any shelf in the warehouse.

6 Put the sentences in the order that they happen in the video (1–5). Compare your answers with a partner.

a The box leaves the warehouse. _____

b The computer tells the workers the correct size of the box. _____

c An Amazon worker finds your item. _____

d You order and pay for an item online. _____

e Your name and address go on the box. _____

⚲ CRITICAL THINKING

7 Work with a partner. Discuss the questions.

APPLY	ANALYZE	EVALUATE
In the future, what jobs will computers do that people do today?	What do you think is the future of physical stores?	Which items are better to buy at a store than online? Why?

COLLABORATION

8 A Work in small groups. Make a business plan for a new business. Include:

- Name
- Product or service
- Location

- Number and type of employees
- Technology
- Marketing / advertising

B Present your business plan to the class. Vote on the best plan.

PEOPLE

LEARNING OBJECTIVES

Key Reading Skill	Using a Venn diagram
Additional Reading Skills	Understanding key vocabulary; scanning to predict content; reading for main ideas; reading for details; taking notes; working out meaning; identifying purpose; previewing; making inferences; synthesizing
Language Development	Noun phrases with *of;* adjectives to describe people

ACTIVATE YOUR KNOWLEDGE

Look at the photos and answer the questions.

What do you think the people in the large photo are like? Describe them.

What are the names of the people in the small photos?

What did they do to become famous?

PREPARING TO READ

1 UNDERSTANDING KEY VOCABULARY **Read the definitions. Complete the sentences with the correct form of the words in bold.**

> **blind** (adj) not able to see
>
> **incredible** (adj) impossible or very diffi cult to believe; amazing
>
> **inspire** (v) to make other people feel that they want to do something
>
> **operation** (n) the process when doctors cut your body to repair it or to take something out
>
> **respect** (v) to like or to have a very good opinion of someone because of their knowledge, achievements, etc.
>
> **talent** (n) a natural ability to do something well

1   After the _____ on his foot, Alex had to stay in the hospital until he could walk on his own.

2   Liz Murray went to Harvard, and then became a best-selling author. It is _____ that she was homeless only a few years before she went to Harvard!

3   Julia was _____ when she was born, so she could not see. Her parents taught her words by putting objects in her hands so she could touch them.

Indra Nooyi, CEO of
PepsiCo, speaking at
the Aspen Ideas Festival

4　Fernanda had a special _____ for playing the piano. She could listen to a song and then play it almost perfectly without any practice.

5　Mahatma Gandhi did a lot of important things for the people of India. I really _____ him and everything he did for people.

6　Having more examples of women as CEOs of businesses will _____ more young girls to reach for similar goals.

2　SCANNING TO PREDICT CONTENT　**Read the title and the first sentence in each paragraph of the blog post on pages 126–127. What do you think the blog post will be about?**

a　someone who helped people with cancer

b　someone who was blind and trained to be a doctor

c　someone who was blind but learned how to see

3　**After you read the blog post, check your answer to Exercise 2.**

A statue of Mahatma Gandhi in London, England

INCREDIBLE
PEOPLE

ABOUT ME

My name is Juliet Selby. I write about people that I <u>admire</u>. I write about a different person every week. Read about their amazing lives here!

ARCHIVE

▶ 2018
▼ 2017
  ▼ <u>Ben Underwood</u>
  ▶ <u>Steve Jobs</u>
  ▶ <u>Mary Evans</u>
▶ 2016
▶ 2015

1 Ben Underwood was a normal teenage boy. He loved playing basketball, riding his bicycle, listening to music with his friends, and playing video games. But in one way, Ben was different from most other teenagers—he was blind. However, Ben had a special **talent**. He didn't have eyes, but he could still "see."

2 Ben was born on January 26, 1992. For the first two years of his life, Ben was a happy and healthy baby. He had a normal life, living with his mother and two older brothers in California. However, when Ben was two years old, his life changed. In 1994, he was taken to the hospital because he had problems with his eyes. The doctors looked at his eyes and told his mother the bad news—Ben had cancer[1]. After a few months, he had an **operation** to remove the cancer. The operation was successful, and Ben was fine. However, the doctors had to remove his eyes, and Ben became **blind**.

3 After his operation, Ben developed an **incredible** talent. When he was three, he learned how to "see" buildings with his ears. He listened very carefully, and he could hear noises bounce off buildings. The noises told him where the buildings were. Then, when Ben was seven, he learned to "click." He made clicking noises with his mouth, and listened for the noises that bounced back from things. In this way, Ben could "see" where he was and what was around him. This is the same way dolphins see things underwater and bats see in the dark.

4 Scientists and doctors were amazed by Ben's talent. There are only a few blind people in the world who can see like Ben. People **respected** him because of this. He became famous. He was on TV, and he traveled to different countries and talked to people about his life. Sadly, when Ben was 16, his cancer came back. He died soon after. However, during Ben's life, he taught people that anything is possible. Many people <u>admired</u> him because he **inspired** them and helped them feel strong. When he died in 2009, over 2,000 people went to his funeral.

¹cancer (n) a serious disease that makes people very sick because cells in the body grow in ways that are not normal or controlled

WHILE READING

4 READING FOR MAIN IDEAS **Read the blog post on pages 126–127. Write the paragraph number where you can find the information below.**

a Ben learned to "see" again. _____

b Ben was an ordinary boy, but he could do something amazing. _____

c Ben became a hero for many people. _____

d Ben became ill and lost his eyes. _____

5 READING FOR DETAILS **Read the blog post again and write *T* (true) or *F* (false) next to the statements. Correct the false statements.**

_____ 1 Ben liked playing basketball.

_____ 2 Ben was just like other teenagers.

_____ 3 Ben learned to "see" by touching things.

_____ 4 Ben couldn't ride a bicycle.

_____ 5 Ben had two older brothers.

_____ 6 Ben liked listening to music.

6 TAKING NOTES **Put the events in Ben's life in the correct order on the timeline.**

a Ben learned how to "see" buildings with his ears.
b Ben was born.
c Ben learned how to "click."
d Ben's cancer came back.
e Ben had a problem with his eyes.
f Ben died.
g Ben went on a TV show.

1   2   3   4   5   6   7

____ ____ ____ ____ ____ ____ ____

READING BETWEEN THE LINES

7 WORKING OUT MEANING **Look at the underlined word in the text, and circle its synonym.**

a dislike b respect c employ

8 IDENTIFYING PURPOSE **Circle the correct answer.**

1 Who do you think wrote the blog?

   a a scientist b a journalist

2 Why do you think the author wrote this blog?

   a to teach doctors about cancer b to tell people the story of Ben's life

CRITICAL THINKING

9 **Discuss the questions with a partner.**

UNDERSTAND	APPLY	ANALYZE
Why did so many people respect Ben? Give at least three reasons.	Describe one person you admire.	Who are three famous children or teenagers? Why are they famous?

COLLABORATION

10 **A** Work with a partner. Choose one famous child or teenager from your list in Exercise 9. Make a list of 10 questions to ask that person in an interview.

• school • hobbies

• work • family

• daily life • friends

B Role-play the interview. One person is the interviewer. The other person is the famous person.

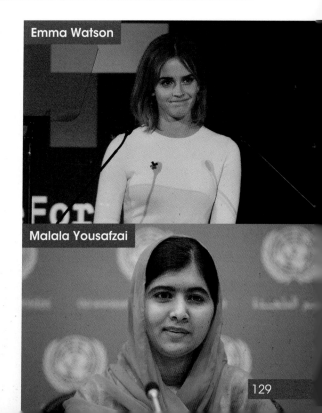

Emma Watson

Malala Yousafzai

PREPARING TO READ

 1 UNDERSTANDING KEY VOCABULARY **Read the sentences and write the words in bold next to the correct definitions.**

1 My mom thinks I'm too young to **take care of** my little sister, so a babysitter comes to my house every day.

2 My **former** job was boring because I sat at my computer all day. At my current job, I talk to a lot of customers, and I like that much better.

3 Aisha runs at least ten miles (16 kilometers) every morning to **train** for the upcoming race.

4 It is important for a president to be **honest**. People must be able to trust the person leading their country.

5 People say Terence Tao is one of the most **intelligent** people in the world. He earned a Ph.D. at only age 20 and became a math professor at age 24

6 Eugene was **brave** when he ran into a burning house to save an elderly woman. He could have died, but he did it anyway.

7 After five tries, 64-year-old Diana Nyad was finally able to **achieve** her goal of swimming from Cuba to Florida. It took her almost 53 hours to finish the 100-mile (160-kilometer) swim.

8 William graduated from college and then decided to follow his **dream** of opening a restaurant.

Terence Tao and other Breakthrough Prize winners

a _____ (n) something that you really want to do, be, or have in the future

b _____ (phr v) to care for or be responsible for someone or something

c _____ (adj) not afraid of dangerous or difficult situations

d _____ (adj) before the present time or in the past

e _____ (adj) able to learn and understand things easily; smart

f _____ (v) to prepare for a job, activity, or sport by learning skills or by exercise

g _____ (adj) truthful or able to be trusted; not likely to lie, cheat, or steal

h _____ (v) to succeed in doing something difficult

2 PREVIEWING **Look at the title, headings, and photos of Reading 2 on pages 132–133. Answer the questions.**

1 What is a *role model*? _____

2 What kind of text is it? _____

3 How many people will you read about? _____

4 Which people do you know about? Write each person's name and one sentence about them.

_____

_____

_____

_____

Diana Nyad

ROLE MODELS

▶ STEVE JOBS

1 I really admire Steve Jobs, the **former** CEO of Apple. He invented a new kind of technology. Apple technology is very **intelligent**, but it is also easy to use. The products that he made are also really beautiful. Steve Jobs is a good role model because he was an excellent businessman. He worked hard, and he created a successful business in IT. I was very sad when he died in October 2011. I respect him because he changed the way people use technology all over the world.

Ahmed Aziz, _____

▶ MARY EVANS

2 My mom, Mary Evans, is my role model. I have a very big family, with two brothers and three sisters. My mom works very hard every day to **take care of** us, and she is very busy. She always makes time for everyone, and she always listens to me if I have a problem. She gives me advice, and she is always right. I have a nephew who is sick and has to go to the hospital a lot. My mom often sleeps at the hospital with him. I really respect her because she always takes care of my family and makes sure that we have everything we need. She is my hero.

Mark Evans, _____

▶ SINGAPORE WOMEN'S EVEREST TEAM

3 My role models are the Singapore Women's Everest Team. In 2009, they became the first all-women team to climb Mount Everest. The team of six young women **trained** for seven years before they climbed the mountain. It was difficult for them to train because Singapore doesn't have any snow or mountains. But they didn't stop, and in the end they **achieved** their goal. They worked hard every day for their **dream**, so I really admire them.

Li Chan, _____

▶ MALALA YOUSAFZAI

4 Malala Yousafzai is a **brave** and **honest** young woman. In Pakistan, the Taliban didn't let girls go to school. Malala went anyway. She wrote a blog for the BBC describing the terrible things the Taliban were doing. In 2012, two men came onto her school bus and shot her in the head. Luckily, Malala survived. She gave speeches about the millions of girls around the world who were not allowed to go to school. In 2014, Malala won the Nobel Peace Prize. She donated her $1.1 million prize money to build a school for girls in Pakistan. Malala is a good role model because she is brave, she never gives up, and she tells the truth no matter what.

Jane Kloster, _____

WHILE READING

 3 READING FOR MAIN IDEAS **Read the texts on pages 132–133. Match the sentence halves.**

1 Steve Jobs

2 Mary Evans

3 The Singapore Women's Everest Team

4 Malala Yousafzai

a takes care of her family.

b fights for girls to go to school.

c invented a new kind of technology.

d climbed a mountain.

4 READING FOR DETAILS **Look at the sentences. There is one mistake in each one. Correct the false information.**

1 In 2009, the Singapore Women's Everest team climbed Everest after five years of training.

2 Malala Yousafzai donated $1.1 million to build a library in Pakistan.

3 Steve Jobs died in June 2011.

4 Mark's mother takes care of his grandmother in the hospital.

READING BETWEEN THE LINES

 5 MAKING INFERENCES **In the text on pages 132–133, the jobs of the people writing the comments have been removed. Write the jobs of the writers next to their names.**

a an explorer
b a student
c an IT technician
d an author

Mt. Everest, Attitude: 29,029 ft (8,848 m)

⚙ SKILLS

USING A VENN DIAGRAM

A *Venn diagram* has two circles that overlap in the middle. You can use Venn diagrams to think about the similarities between people or ideas. Venn diagrams help organize the qualities that people or ideas share. To complete a Venn diagram, write the shared qualities of people or ideas in the overlapping section of the circles.

6 TAKING NOTES **Compare two people from Reading 2. Take notes on each person in the outside sections, and write their shared qualities in the middle.**

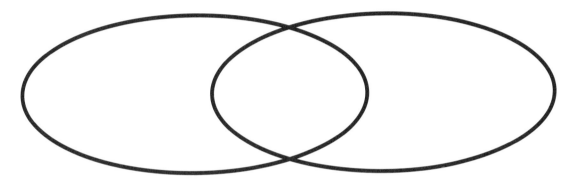

☀ CRITICAL THINKING

7 SYNTHESIZING **Work with a partner. Use ideas from Reading 1 and Reading 2 to discuss the questions.**

APPLY	ANALYZE	EVALUATE
Who are the most famous people in your country?	How can famous people inspire others to do good things?	Think about the people in Unit 7. Who are you the most similar to? Explain.

👥 COLLABORATION

8 A Work in small groups. Make a T-chart. Write at least five advantages and five disadvantages of fame.

B Separate the class into two groups. One side will argue that fame is positive. The other group will argue that fame is negative.

C Have a class debate. Your teacher will decide who wins.

LANGUAGE DEVELOPMENT

NOUN PHRASES WITH *OF*

1 **Look at the noun phrases in the second column, and match the sentence halves.**

1	A chair is	**a**	the principal of the school.
2	I travel to	**b**	the beginning of the day.
3	A dog is	**c**	a kind of furniture.
4	Coffee is	**d**	a lot of countries.
5	Write your name at	**e**	a sort of drink.
6	My teacher is	**f**	the top of the page.
7	We eat breakfast at	**g**	a type of animal.

2 **Put the words in order to make complete sentences.**

1 the new leader / She / of / the country / is / .

_____

2 of / I met / my brother's / a friend / .

_____

3 gave me / of / a piece / My mother / cake / .

_____

4 a kind / A dentist / doctor / is / of / .

_____

5 of / the former director / is / technology / He / .

_____

ADJECTIVES TO DESCRIBE PEOPLE

3 Are the adjectives in the box positive or negative? Write the words in the correct place in the table. Some answers may fit in both columns. Use a dictionary to look up any words you don't know.

> reliable   confident   lazy   honest   calm   talented
> kind   shy   intelligent   patient   stupid
> clever   difficult   sensible   selfish   friendly

positive	negative

4 Use adjectives from Exercise 3 to complete the sentences.

1   Luka is very ——————— . He always tells the truth.

2   My teacher is ——————— . She is very relaxed and doesn't get worried or angry.

3   She always chats with students in other classes. She's so ——————— .

4   She doesn't talk very much. She's really ——————— .

5   James hasn't done anything all day. He's so ——————— .

6   Ahmed is very ——————— . He always comes to work on time and does his job.

7   Dae-Jung is practical and doesn't do anything stupid. He's very ——————— .

8   He is a very ——————— driver. He wins every race easily.

WATCH AND LISTEN

PREPARING TO WATCH

1 ACTIVATING YOUR KNOWLEDGE **Work with a partner and answer the questions.**

1 What is a volunteer?

2 Why do people become volunteers?

3 Where do volunteers work?

2 PREDICTING CONTENT USING VISUALS **Work with your partner. Look at the pictures from the video. What kind of work do you think the man is doing?**

WHILE WATCHING

3 UNDERSTANDING MAIN IDEAS **Read the sentences. Then watch the video. Write *T* (true) or *F* (false). Correct the false statements.**

_____ 1 850 volunteers record the weather in the U.S. every day.

_____ 2 Richard Hendrickson is a volunteer for the National Weather Service.

_____ 3 He monitors the temperature from his kitchen.

_____ 4 This job is difficult for him.

_____ 5 Richard also checks the snowfall daily.

_____ 6 He uses his cell phone to call the National Weather Service.

_____ 7 The National Weather Service will honor him for his time as a volunteer.

4 UNDERSTANDING DETAILS **Watch again. Choose the correct answer.**

1   Richard Hendrickson is _____ years old.

   a 85   **b** 90   **c** 101

2   He lives in _____, New York.

   a Bridgehampton   **b** Brooklyn   **c** Long Beach

3   He started recording the weather in _____.

   a 1925   **b** 1930   **c** 1940

4   Weather was important to him because he was _____.

   a an engineer   **b** a farmer   **c** a teacher

5 MAKING INFERENCES **Work with a partner. Discuss the questions.**

1   Why do you think Richard first became a volunteer?
2   Will he stop volunteering for the National Weather Service?

⌾ CRITICAL THINKING

6 **Work in small groups. Discuss the questions.**

APPLY	ANALYZE	EVALUATE
What kind of volunteer work have you done or would you like to do?	What kind of volunteer work would you not like to do? Why?	What are five personal benefits of being a volunteer?

COLLABORATION

7 **A**   Work with a partner. Which of the following is the most important way to achieve success? Put them in order of importance, and explain your reasons. Then add two more things to your list.

   • having talent   • helping others   • overcoming difficulties

B   Work with another pair. Compare your lists. Discuss your reasons, and agree on a new list and order of importance.

C   Repeat step B as a class.

THE UNIVERSE

LEARNING OBJECTIVES

Key Reading Skill	Identifying the author's purpose
Additional Reading Skills	Understanding key vocabulary; using your knowledge; previewing; reading for main ideas; reading for details; scanning to predict content; annotating; making inferences; distinguishing fact from opinion; synthesizing
Language Development	Giving evidence and supporting an argument; infinitives of purpose

ACTIVATE YOUR KNOWLEDGE

Look at the photo and answer the questions.

1 Do you ever look at the night sky? Why?

2 In your opinion, is there life on other planets?

3 Why do governments send people to space?

4 Would you like to travel to space? Why or why not?

READING 1

1 UNDERSTANDING KEY VOCABULARY **Read the sentences. Write the words in bold next to the definitions on page 143.**

1 Mariam loves to **explore** new places. She even wants to travel to Mars one day to learn about it.

2 Thanks to developing technology, **advances** in science and medicine are made all the time.

3 Astronauts have not set foot **beyond** the moon, but one day soon they may go to planets that are farther away.

4 It is important for an **entrepreneur** to understand that they might lose all of their money if their new business fails.

5 The rocket **crashed** when it was landing. Luckily, the people inside were not hurt.

6 Tesla is a **private** company. The government does not run it.

7 Some people don't think we should use **public** money, like taxes, to pay for space travel. They think companies should pay for it.

a _____ (n) someone who starts their own business

b _____ (n) progress in the development or improvement of something

c _____ (adj) related to money or services controlled or supplied by a person or a company and not by the government

d _____ (v) to travel to a new place to learn about it

e _____ (prep) on the farther side of; at a farther distance than

f _____ (v) to hit something by accident, especially in a vehicle

g _____ (adj) related to money or services controlled or supplied by the government and not by a person or a company

2 USING YOUR KNOWLEDGE **Work with a partner. Answer the questions.**

1 Who usually pays for space exploration?

_____

2 Do you think people will ever vacation in space? Why or why not?

_____

_____

_____

3 PREVIEWING **Look at the title, subtitle, and photos in the article on pages 144–145. Answer the questions.**

1 Where would you find this text? _____

_____

2 What is the "New Space Race"? _____

_____

3 Who is Elon Musk? _____

_____

4 Who is Richard Branson? _____

_____

The New Space Race:

THE RISE OF COMMERCIAL[1] SPACE TRAVEL

Elon Musk and *Dragon*

1 In 1957, the Soviet Union sent *Sputnik I* into space. It was the first successful spacecraft to orbit[2] the Earth, and it started the time period known as the Space Age. A short time later in the U.S., the National Aeronautics Space Administration (NASA) successfully sent another spacecraft, *Explorer I*, into space. In the years that followed, incredible **advances** were made. Astronauts orbited the Earth and men walked on the moon. The world, it seemed, wanted to learn what was **beyond** Earth.

> **"** ⸻
> **The world, it seemed, wanted to learn what was beyond Earth.**

2 Today, space exploration continues, and governments still compete with one another to make new discoveries. In 2012, NASA landed its unmanned[3] spacecraft *Curiosity* on Mars in order to collect information about the planet. In 2016, Europe and Russia worked together and sent a spacecraft to Mars. China and India are also working on similar projects. However, there has been one big change: **private** companies, instead of **public** government organizations, are entering the Space Race.

3 SpaceX has been very successful in commercial space travel. They designed the spacecraft *Dragon* in order to deliver supplies to the International Space Station (ISS). In 2012, *Dragon* was the first commercial spacecraft in history to do that. Elon Musk, the man who started the company, has dreams that go beyond making deliveries. He hopes that SpaceX will be able to send people to Mars by 2025.

4 Another **entrepreneur** who supports commercial space travel is Richard Branson. He started a private company called Virgin Galactic. Their goal is to open space travel to everyone. The company has sold almost 700

Virgin Galactic's VSS Enterprise

future trips to space, at the high cost of $250,000 per person. Those future space tourists come from countries all over the world and are all different ages.

5 Private companies are lucky in one way. They don't have to wait for money from the government like NASA does. However, that doesn't mean that setbacks[4] and accidents don't happen. In 2014, Virgin Galactic's *VSS Enterprise* **crashed** in the Mojave Desert during a test flight. The 39-year-old pilot, Michael Alsbury, was killed. In 2016, a SpaceX spacecraft that was going to the ISS exploded on the launch pad in Cape Canaveral, Florida. No one was hurt, but important supplies were lost.

> " The race to explore the universe continues, and many private companies are competing.

Richard Branson and a Virgin Galactic spacecraft

6 The race to **explore** the universe continues, and many private companies are competing. Some of those companies want to take people to the moon and back someday. Others want to take people to Mars. The possibilities are endless. Maybe in our lifetime, those dreams will come true.

[1]**commercial** (adj) with the purpose of making money

[2]**orbit** (v) to travel in a circular journey around the sun, the moon, or a planet

[3]**unmanned** (adj) without people to operate something or make something work properly

[4]**setbacks** (n) problems that make something happen later or more slowly than it should

4 READING FOR MAIN IDEAS **Read the article on pages 144–145 and answer the questions.**

1 What is the Space Age?
2 What are countries competing with one another for?
3 What are some goals of future space travel?
4 What is one difference between public and private companies?

5 READING FOR DETAILS **Read the statements. Write *T* (true), *F* (false), or *DNS* (does not say). Then correct the false statements.**

_____ 1 NASA sent *Sputnik I* into space, and it was the first successful spacecraft to orbit the Earth.

_____ 2 Entrepreneurs like Elon Musk and Richard Branson have to wait for government money in order to construct new spacecraft.

_____ 3 In 2016, a SpaceX spacecraft exploded in Cape Canaveral, Florida, and killed its pilot.

_____ 4 Virgin Galactic has sold nearly 500 future trips to space.

_____ 5 Elon Musk also runs an innovative car company.

READING BETWEEN THE LINES

⚒ SKILLS

IDENTIFYING THE AUTHOR'S PURPOSE

Authors write in order to inform, explain, entertain, or persuade readers. The author's purpose may be understood by his or her use of key words, tone, and language in the text. Good readers identify why a text was written. The author's purpose may be stated clearly in the text, or it may have to be inferred.

6 IDENTIFYING PURPOSE **Read the article again. Circle the correct answers.**

1 The purpose of the text is to …
   a persuade readers that commercial space travel is necessary.
   b inform readers about the advances in commercial space travel.
   c entertain readers about the possibility of life on Mars.

2   The author is …

   a   analyzing commercial space travel.

   b   describing commercial space travel.

   c   questioning the benefits of commercial space travel.

⚙ CRITICAL THINKING

7   Discuss the questions with a partner.

ANALYZE

Would you pay a lot of money to be a space tourist? Why or why not?

EVALUATE

Why might some people want to leave Earth and live on Mars?

⚙ COLLABORATION

8 **A** Work in small groups. Create a survey about people's interest in space and space travel. Write at least six more questions in the chart.

	Yes	No
1 Would you like to visit Mars?		
2		
3		
4		
5		
6		
7		

B Each member of your group will ask five people the survey questions and record the answers.

C Summarize the results of your group's survey. Present your results to the class.

Our Future on Mars?

READING 2

1 UNDERSTANDING KEY VOCABULARY **Circle the best definition for each word in bold.**

1 I often **wonder** if people will travel to Mars one day. Maybe NASA will send someone there in the next ten or fifteen years.

   a think about something and try to understand it

   b not believe something

2 My essay is weak because I didn't **support** my ideas with expert opinions. I should find more research to add to my essay.

   a think of more topics to write about

   b help show that something is true

3 A lot of **evidence** shows that Mars once had flowing water.

   a opinions that people have about a topic

   b something that makes you believe something is true

4 Scientists have been studying space for many years. Some think there is life on other planets, but no one can **prove** it.

   a show that something is true

   b ask questions about something

5 Life can't **exist** without air and water. For that reason, Earth is the perfect planet for life.

   a be real, alive, or present

   b have ideas

6 Because it was so difficult, Elise thought it was **unlikely** that she would pass her astronomy class.

   a would probably happen

   b not expected to happen; not probable

7 Astronauts have to train a lot in order to prepare for the **conditions** they'll face in space, such as very hot and very cold temperatures.

   a the location of something

   b the physical state that someone or something is in

8 On **particular** nights, you can see the brightest planets when you look at the sky. That only happens when the sky is clear.

   a used to talk about one thing or person and not others

   b many different

2 USING YOUR KNOWLEDGE **Answer the questions with a partner.**

1 How many planets are there in our solar system? Name them.

_____

_____

_____

2 Do you think there is life on other planets? Why or why not?

_____

_____

_____

3 SCANNING TO PREDICT CONTENT **Read the title and the first sentence of each paragraph of the text on pages 150–151. What type of text is it?**

a a story   b an essay   c a newspaper article

Is There Life on **Other Planets**?

1 For many years, people have **wondered** whether we are the only living things in the universe. Some scientists believe that there must be life on other planets because the universe is so big. However, it is **unlikely** that there is life on other planets because planets need a very specific environment for life to start. In the end, there are no facts that **support** the idea of life on other planets.

Kepler telescope

Kepler 22b

2 First of all, it is true that the universe is huge. It has billions of stars and thousands of solar systems. As of 2016, experts using the very powerful Kepler telescope[1] have found more than 2,300 planets in orbit around stars. A lot of these planets are similar to Earth. In fact, a number of scientists believe that one of these planets, named Kepler 22b, has the right **conditions**—the right atmosphere[2] and temperature—to support life. However, there is no **evidence** that there is life on Kepler 22b. Experts with the best technology can see no signs of life there. Until there is hard evidence, we cannot use Kepler 22b to support the idea of life on other planets.

An observatory

3 A planet needs very **particular** conditions to support life. A planet with life would need to have water, the right temperature, and the right mix of chemicals in the atmosphere. Earth has the perfect conditions for life, and it is highly unlikely that another planet has exactly the same environment as Earth. In addition, although scientists believe that life might **exist** on other planets, they have never found evidence to **prove** it. A recent report from Princeton University suggests that it is highly unlikely that there is life on other planets. The researchers believe that we don't have enough scientific evidence to decide if there is life on other planets. They say that just because conditions similar to Earth exist on other planets, it doesn't mean that life exists there.

4 In conclusion, I do not believe that there is life on other planets. Although the universe is very big, a planet with life needs very special conditions. Earth has exactly the right conditions for life. It is not too hot or too cold. It has water, air, and the right chemicals. I do not think that any other planets could have exactly the same conditions as Earth. Therefore, I do not think that there could be life on other planets.

[1]telescope (n) a piece of equipment, in the shape of a tube, that makes things that are far away look bigger or nearer

[2]atmosphere (n) the layer of gases around a planet

4 READING FOR MAIN IDEAS **Read the text on pages 150–151. Write the number of the paragraph where the author mentions each idea.**

a There is not enough evidence to prove that Kepler 22b has life. ____

b Earth is the only planet with the right conditions for life. ____

c There are arguments for and against the idea that life exists on other planets. ____

d It is unlikely that there is life on another planet because the conditions for life to exist are too particular. ____

5 ANNOTATING **Read the questions. Find and highlight the answers in Reading 2. Then write the answers in the blanks.**

1 How many solar systems are there in the universe? _____

2 What is the name of the telescope that discovers new planets? _____

3 What is Kepler 22b? _____

4 Which university wrote a report saying that it is unlikely that there is life on other planets? _____

5 What does the author say we need before we can know if there is life on other planets? _____

READING BETWEEN THE LINES

6 MAKING INFERENCES **Why do you think Kepler 22b was given its name?**

7 DISTINGUISHING FACT FROM OPINION **Read the sentences from the text. Which are facts and which are opinions? Write *F* (fact) or *O* (opinion).**

1 There must be life on other planets. _____

2 The universe has billions of stars and thousands of solar systems. _____

3 It is highly unlikely that there is life on other planets. _____

4 A planet needs very particular conditions to support life. _____

8 IDENTIFYING PURPOSE **Read the questions and circle the correct answers.**

1   What is the author's main purpose?

   a to entertain readers

   b to make readers agree with his or her opinion

   c to inform readers

2   What does the author believe?

   a The universe is so big that there must be life on other planets.

   b Life probably doesn't exist on other planets.

   c Life most likely exists on other planets; we just have to find it.

3   Why does the author include information from a recent report from Princeton University?

   a to prove that experts agree with his or her opinion

   b to show that there are two sides to the argument

   c to prove that life exists on other planets

⌁ CRITICAL THINKING

9 SYNTHESIZING **Work with a partner. Use ideas from Reading 1 and Reading 2 to answer the questions.**

ANALYZE

Will private companies make it possible for tourists to go to the moon or to explore planets like Mars or Kepler 22b? Why or why not?

EVALUATE

Would private companies help us learn more about other planets and their environments? Why or why not?

⚙ COLLABORATION

10 A Space exploration has led to many inventions. With a partner, rank these inventions in order of importance from *1* (most important) to *6* (least important). Explain your reasons.

   • microcomputers

   • GPS navigation

   • satellite TV

   • electric cars

   • robotic arms

   • freeze-dried food

   B Share your rankings with another group. Discuss your reasons, and agree on a final order of rankings.

   C Repeat step B as a class.

GIVING EVIDENCE AND SUPPORTING AN ARGUMENT

> **LANGUAGE**
>
> In an essay, arguments are supported with evidence. The nouns *research, study, expert,* and *report* are used to support arguments. Writers use the verbs *think* or *believe* for a person, and the verbs *show* or *suggest* for a piece of work.

1 **Read the sentences. Write the underlined nouns next to the definitions. One definition has two correct answers.**

1 The psychology student is doing <u>research</u> about memory loss.
2 I had to read an interesting <u>study</u> about fish for my biology class.
3 His mother works for the city as a public transportation <u>expert</u>.
4 The American Heart Association published a <u>report</u> last week about the dangers of smoking.

a _____ _____ (n) someone who has a lot of skill in something or a lot of knowledge about something

b _____ _____ (n) a document that tells us about a subject in detail

c _____ _____ (n) the study of a subject to discover new information

the Milky Way

2 **Complete the sentences with the correct verbs from the box. More than one answer is possible.**

believe   show   suggest   think

1 Experts _____ that the moon is too cold for people to live there.

2 Studies _____ that there are over 200 billion stars in the Milky Way galaxy.

3 Scientists _____ that we need to study space.

4 Reports _____ that parts of Mars were once covered in ice.

5 Research _____ that there could be 50 billion planets in our galaxy.

INFINITIVES OF PURPOSE

> **LANGUAGE**
>
> Writers use *in order to* + the base form of the verb to express a purpose, or why something is done.
>
> NASA sent robots to Mars **in order to find** water.
>
> Writers *use to* + the base form of the verb alone when the meaning is clear.
>
> SpaceX designed Dragon **(in order) to find** water.

3 **Match the sentence halves.**

1 We build rockets

2 We sent the International Space Station into space

3 We went to the moon

a (in order) to explore it in more detail.

b (in order) to send people into space.

c (in order) to find out if people could live in space.

4 **Complete the sentences in three different ways using infinitives of purpose.**

1 We explore space (in order) to _____.

2 We explore space (in order) to _____.

3 We explore space (in order) to _____.

WATCH AND LISTEN

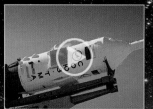   

GLOSSARY

astronaut (n) someone who travels to and works in space

International Space Station (n) the name of an international spacecraft where astronauts work on projects

rocket (n) a vehicle for traveling to space

capsule (n) the part of the rocket where the astronauts are

blast off (phr v) to leave the ground; for example, when a spacecraft or rocket blasts off, it leaves the ground.

PREPARING TO WATCH

1 ACTIVATING YOUR KNOWLEDGE **Work with a partner and answer the questions.**

1 How do people usually get to work when they live far from their workplace?

2 Why might people live far from their workplace?

3 What are some unusual offices or workplaces?

2 USING YOUR KNOWLEDGE **You are going to watch a video about a woman who traveled to space for work. Write five adjectives and five nouns to describe a trip to space.**

Adjectives: _____ , _____ , _____ , _____ , _____

Nouns: _____ , _____ , _____ , _____ , _____

WHILE WATCHING

3 UNDERSTANDING MAIN IDEAS **Watch the video. Answer the questions.**

1 What does Sunita Williams do? _____

2 What is the name of her office in space? _____

3 How did she get there? _____

4 What was not a problem when she went there? _____

5 What took longer, her trip to space or her drive to work? _____

▶ **4** UNDERSTANDING DETAILS **Watch again. Complete the sentences with the correct numbers.**

1 It takes Sunita Williams _____ minutes to drive to the office.

2 She drives her car _____ miles to the offi ce in Houston, Texas.

3 She spent _____ months in space.

4 The trip to space was _____ miles straight up.

5 The trip took _____ minutes.

5 **Correct the mistakes in the sentences. Compare your answers with a partner.**

1 The rocket is American.
2 The trip took double the time it takes her to drive to work.
3 She traveled in a big capsule.
4 She went with a Russian cosmonaut and a Korean astronaut.
5 They rode the elevator to the bottom.

☼ CRITICAL THINKING

6 **Work with a partner. Discuss the questions.**

APPLY	ANALYZE	EVALUATE
What are the dangers of traveling to space?	What kind of person works in space?	Would you prefer to explore space, the ocean, or the Amazon rain forest? Why?

COLLABORATION

7 **A** Work in groups of five. Prepare a role play. Each person will play one of the following people in a roundtable discussion.

- the head of the national space program
- the principal of a poor public school
- a private citizen and tax payer
- a scientist
- an environmentalist

Think about your role. Would you agree or disagree with the following statement?

The government should spend more money on space exploration.

B Do the role play as a roundtable discussion.

GLOSSARY OF KEY VOCABULARY

Words that are part of the Academic Word List are noted with an (A) in this glossary.

UNIT 1 PLACES

READING 1

capital (n) the most important city in a country or state; where the government is

countryside (n) land that is not in towns or cities and may have farms and fields

expert (A) (n) someone who has a lot of skill in or a lot of knowledge about something

modern (adj) designed and made using the most recent ideas and methods

opportunity (n) a chance to do or experience something good

pollution (n) damage caused to water, air, and land by harmful materials or waste

population (n) the number of people living in a place

traffic (n) the cars, trucks, and other vehicles using a road

READING 2

area (A) (n) a region or part of a larger place, like a country or city

cheap (adj) not expensive, or costs less than usual

downtown (adj) the main or central part of a city

expensive (adj) costs a lot of money; not cheap

local (adj) relating to a particular area, city, or town

noisy (adj) loud; makes a lot of noise

quiet (adj) makes little or no noise

UNIT 2 FESTIVALS AND CELEBRATIONS

READING 1

celebrate (v) to do something enjoyable because it is a special day

culture (A) (n) the habits, traditions, and beliefs of a country or group of people

gift (n) something that you give to someone, usually on a special day

the ground (n) the surface of the Earth

lucky (adj) having good things happen to you

traditional (A) (adj) following the ways of behaving or doing things that have continued in a group of people for a long time

READING 2

activity (n) something people do for fun

highlight (A) (n) the most enjoyable part of something

history (n) the whole series of events in the past that relate to the development of a country, subject, or person

popular (adj) liked by many people

take part in (phr v) to do an activity with other people

visitor (n) someone who goes to see a person or a place

UNIT 3 THE INTERNET AND TECHNOLOGY

READING 1

benefit Ⓐ (n) a good or helpful result or effect

collect (v) to get things from different places and bring them together

free (adj) costing no money

interest (n) something you enjoy doing or learning about

record (v) to store sounds, pictures, or information on a camera or computer so that they can be used in the future

secret (adj) not known or seen by other people

security Ⓐ (n) the things that are done to keep someone or something safe

software (n) programs you use to make a computer do different things

READING 2

affect Ⓐ (v) to influence someone or something; to cause change

creative Ⓐ (adj) good at thinking of new ideas or creating new and unusual things

download (v) to copy computer programs, music, or other information electronically from the Internet to your computer

educational (adj) providing education, or relating to education

imagination (n) the part of your mind that creates ideas or pictures of things that are not real or that you have not seen

improve (v) to get better or to make something better

UNIT 4 WEATHER AND CLIMATE

READING 1

almost (adv) not everything, but very close to it

cover (v) to lie on the surface of something

dangerous (adj) can harm or hurt someone or something

huge (adj) extremely large in size or amount

last (v) to continue for a period of time

lightning (n) a flash of bright light in the sky during a storm

thunder (n) the sudden loud noise that comes after a flash of lightning

READING 2

careful (adj) paying attention to what you are doing so that you do not have an accident, make a mistake, or damage something

decide (v) to choose between one possibility or another

drop (v) to decrease; to fall or go down

precipitation (n) rain or snow that falls to the ground

rise (v) to increase; to go up

shock (n) a big, unpleasant surprise

UNIT 5 SPORTS AND COMPETITION

ancient (adj) from a long time ago; very old

compete (v) to take part in a race or competition; to try to be more successful than someone else

competition (n) an organized event in which people try to win a prize by being the best

strange (adj) not familiar; difficult to understand; different

swimming (n) a sport where people move through water by moving their body

take place (phr v) to happen

throw (v) to send something through the air, pushing it out of your hand

accident (n) something bad that happens that is not intended and that causes injury or damage

challenging Ⓐ (adj) difficult in a way that tests your ability

climb (v) to go up something or onto the top of something, like a tree or mountain

course (n) an area used for sports events, such as racing or playing golf

in shape (adj) in good health; strong

participant Ⓐ (n) someone who takes part in an activity

UNIT 6 BUSINESS

apply (v) to ask officially for something, often by writing

colleague Ⓐ (n) someone that you work with

customer (n) someone who buys things from a store or business

occupation Ⓐ (n) a job or career

organize (v) to plan or arrange carefully

result (n) information that you find out from something, such as an exam, a scientific experiment, or a medical test

advertise (v) to tell people about a product or service, for example in newspapers or on television, in order to persuade them to buy it

employ (v) to pay someone to work or do a job for you

goal Ⓐ (n) something you want to do successfully in the future

introduce (v) to make something available to buy or use for the first time

office (n) a place in a building where people work

partner (n) someone who runs or owns a business with another person

run (v) to manage or operate something

set up (phr v) to create or establish (something) for a particular purpose

UNIT 7 PEOPLE

READING 1

blind (adj) not able to see

incredible (adj) impossible or very difficult to believe; amazing

inspire (v) to make other people feel that they want to do something

operation (n) the process when doctors cut your body to repair it or to take something out

respect (v) to like or to have a very good opinion of someone because of their knowledge, achievements, etc.

talent (n) a natural ability to do something well

READING 2

achieve Ⓐ (v) to succeed in doing something difficult

brave (adj) not afraid of dangerous or difficult situations

dream (n) something that you really want to do, be, or have in the future

former (adj) before the present time or in the past

honest (adj) truthful or able to be trusted; not likely to lie, cheat, or steal

intelligent Ⓐ (adj) able to learn and understand things easily; smart

take care of (phr v) to care for or be responsible for someone or something

train (v) to prepare for a job, activity, or sport by learning skills or by exercise

UNIT 8 THE UNIVERSE

READING 1

advance (n) progress in the development or improvement of something

beyond (prep) on the farther side of; at a farther distance than

crash (v) to hit something by accident, especially in a vehicle

entrepreneur (n) someone who starts their own business

explore (v) to travel to a new place to learn about it

private (adj) related to money or services controlled or supplied by a person or a company and not by the government

public (adj) related to money or services controlled or supplied by the government and not by a person or a company

READING 2

condition (n) the physical state that someone or something is in

evidence Ⓐ (n) something that makes you believe something is true

exist (v) to be real, alive, or present

particular (adj) used to talk about one thing or person and not others

prove (v) to show that something is true

support (v) to help show that something is true

unlikely (adj) not expected to happen; not probable

wonder (v) to think about something and try to understand it

VIDEO SCRIPTS

UNIT 1

▶ The Top U.S. City

Reporter: Called the Holy City, for its many church steeples, peaked above the city's low-slung skyline, it beat out San Francisco, which had won the award 18 years in a row. I think people, at times, are surprised to hear that. Charleston Mayor, Joe Riley.

Joe Riley: Well, you know, when people come to Charleston, whether they're from the U.S. or from another continent, for the first time, they're always surprised. It's like they didn't know this kind of place existed in America.

Reporter: Charleston was a cradle of the Confederacy. It was here the first shots of the Civil War were fired. That history can be felt all around, from streets paved in stones, once used as ballast in sailing ships, to centuries-old houses that line the battery, to the city market, where vendors still sell their handmade crafts. And that doesn't even touch on the great southern cuisine. These are the draws for visitors to Charleston, where the thrill rides don't occur on twisting scream machines, but rather on more sedate vehicles.

Joe Riley: We regulate very carefully the tourism industry. We regulate the number of carriages, where they go. We regulate where buses can go. We regulate the size of walking tours.

Reporter: All that attention to tourism is because it's big business here. 4 million visitors pump more than 3 billion dollars a year into the local economy.

Tom Doyle: Here we go.

Reporter: Tom Doyle has been leading carriage tours in Charleston for more than 30 years.
The attention that Charleston is getting right now, does that surprise you?

Tom Doyle: Uh, no, it doesn't. It surprises me it took as long as it did.
You can go down any street here, look to your left and look to your right and see even more beautiful streets. You can make Charleston your own special place. Isn't this a great city?

Reporter: It's beautiful, I have to say.

UNIT 2

▶ The Meaning of Independence Day

Reporter: To kick off your Fourth of July celebration, how 'bout a little trip to Philadelphia, home of the Second Continental Congress. We found some young Americans in Philly who are learning about the nation's early days from some rather familiar faces.

Men: We hold these truths to be self-evident, that all men are created equal.

Man 1: The Fourth of July is very significant. It is the date upon which we approved the Declaration of Independence.

Woman: I believe that it symbolizes the great unity of our colonies, our collective effort to create our own constellation, our own country.

Young man 1: I think of collaboration, I think of, uh, kind of the best of America, where people—well, the delegates debated together and they really wanted to send a strong message to Britain.
It's really—you know, it's a great day to be American.

Boy 1: Well, I like all the fireworks, and all that's really fun and stuff.

Girl 1: Fireworks.

Girl 2: Our neighbors, like, buy like whole entire box of fireworks, and then they take them and they put them by the sewer and they light them.

Boy 2: Well, the fireworks and it's really fun, but it's like remembering all the people that laid down their lives for us.

Young woman: And I think it's such an important day for us as a nation to celebrate and remember every year. And I think it's so uniting too, to really remember what we were founded on and how blessed we are as a nation.

Young man 2: The sacrifice it took to make this nation and the opportunity we have that many people around the world don't have to life, liberty, and the pursuit of happiness. It's really a neat opportunity to remember how blessed we are to be in this country.

UNIT 3

▶ Predictive Advertising

Narrator: Every time we make a phone call, search online, or buy something, we leave information, or data, about our habits. And the amount of data is getting bigger by 2.5 billion gigabytes every day. All that data is worth a lot of money.

Mike Baker is a "data hunter." He collects data. He thinks this information is changing the way we live and the way we do business.

A few years ago, Mike decided to help advertisers. Why should companies wait for people to find their ads when it was now possible to bring personalized ads to everyone?

Then he had another idea. If companies had enough information about people's past activities, could they use this information to predict their future activities?

Mike felt that they could—that they could predict what people might want to buy. But it was difficult because there was too much data. He needed a program to understand and use the data.

And he wanted to be able to use the data fast—to be able to predict what people wanted to buy, before they even knew it. But he needed help.

So Mike found a partner with a superfast program. Together, they made the program do what Mike wanted it to do. The program looks at data very quickly and finds clues about what people might want to buy.

Then it sends them personalized ads. For example, it might learn that you like Italian food and are interested in cars, so it sends you ads about those things.

We now live in a world of personalized ads. Yes, you can choose not to have personalized ads, but you can't get away from ads completely. So maybe it's better to see ads for things you like than for things you don't care about.

UNIT 4

▶ Tornadoes

Narrator: In the middle of the United States, spring brings warm, wet air from the south, making things perfect for one of the most extreme weather events on Earth—tornadoes. That's why this part of the country is called Tornado Alley.

Some years are worse than others, and 2011 was one of the worst ever.

Man: Did you see that? The whole house came apart! Oh my God! Oh my God!

Narrator: That year, in the town of Joplin, Missouri, a dangerous tornado killed more than 160 people.

But although we know a lot about the science of tornadoes, we still can't predict exactly when or where they will happen.

Josh Wurman is a weather scientist. He and his team are studying how thunderstorms produce tornadoes.

Seventy-five percent of thunderstorms don't produce tornadoes, but twenty-five percent of them do. But which thunderstorms will do it?

To answer this question, Josh and his team need to get information from as many tornadoes as they can during the spring. To find the storms, Josh uses a Doppler radar scanner. It can show him what's going on inside a thunderstorm, which gives him important information about what starts a tornado.

Josh now knows where to look, but finding the right storm is always difficult. Then, after 1,000 miles of driving, they find the right one. But the team has to move fast because tornadoes come and go very quickly.

And there's the tornado they're looking for.

Woman: There we go. That's what it's about.

Man 1: Yeah.

Man 2: There she is.

Man 1: It's a beauty.

Man 2: It's a beauty.

Man on radio: Be careful. Be careful.

Narrator: This huge tornado is less than a mile away from the team.

Its winds are spinning up to 200 miles per hour.

But less than 30 minutes after the tornado appeared, it dies. It was one of more than 1,200 tornadoes in this part of Tornado Alley since the beginning of spring.

UNIT 5

▶ Skiing in the French Alps

Narrator: This is Courchevel, France. It's popular with skiers. There are four villages, and the names tell you the height in meters, like Courchevel 1,300 and Courchevel 1,850, which is the highest most well-known. Rich and famous people, like the American movie star Leonardo DiCaprio, ski here.

In slalom skiing, skiers race between the red and blue flags. The slalom course is in the highest village. Emma Carrick-Anderson is a British skier. She competed in the Winter Olympics.

Dallas Campbell isn't an Olympic skier. But he's ready to race.

Ski official: Left course ready, right course ready, and go!

Narrator: In an Olympic race, the difference between first and tenth place is often less than one second.

We're going to see how to prepare skis to make them go as fast as possible in the snow.

First, they "grind" the bottom of the skis to make them smooth.

Next, they use a special wax to fill in the holes. Then, they make the skis smooth again.

Now his skis are prepared, and Dallas is ready to race Emma again.

Ski official: Yeah, go.

Dallas Campbell: Ah-ha. Ah.

UNIT 6

▶ Amazon's Fulfillment Center

Narrator: Today Amazon is the world's largest online store. But its first warehouse was a small basement in Seattle, Washington.

Now, with more than 100 million items for sale on its website, Amazon has many large warehouses around the world called "fulfillment centers." How do they find your item? Only the central computer knows where everything is. Any item can be on any shelf.

In fact, their location is random so that workers don't take the wrong item.

After you order and pay for an item online, an Amazon worker walks through the warehouse and finds your kitchen item or your cute toy.

The computer then tells the workers the right size of the box.

Finally, your name and address goes on the box before it leaves the fulfillment center.

UNIT 7

▶ **The 101-Year-Old Weather Volunteer**

Reporter: Across the country, 8,500 volunteer observers record the nation's weather every day, but none has been doing it longer than 101-year-old Richard Hendrickson.

Richard: Right now, it is exactly 80.

Reporter: For 84 years now, Hendrickson's been monitoring the highs and lows from the thermometer shelter in his backyard in Bridgehampton, New York. Is this pretty much the way it's always been?

Richard: Oh, yeah.

Reporter: Real simple.

Richard: Just like that. You're getting to show age a little bit here in the joints.

Reporter: We all do.

Richard: Like we all get.

Reporter: He also checks the rainfall daily. And then glances out his dining room window to check the wind.

Richard: It's clear. There's not a cloud in the sky.

Reporter: Before calling it all in on his rotary phone …

Richard: Yeah, Bridgehampton.

Reporter: … to the National Weather Service.

Richard: The sky is clear. The wind is out of the southwest.

Reporter: When Hendrickson started recording the weather in 1930, at age 18, Herbert Hoover was president. This is your journal from the '30s.

Richard: Sure I remember this thing. I'll be damned. In 1933. January. Clear and warm.

Reporter: Weather was important to you because you were a farmer.

Richard: Because I was a livestock farmer.

Reporter: This weekend, the National Weather Service will honor his eight decades as an observer.

Richard: Am I what? Excited? Oh, yeah, sure. I can hardly talk.

Reporter: He does it for his country, Richard Hendrickson says. Collecting the statistics that to this 101-year-old farmer are still just the facts of life.

UNIT 8

▶ **Going to the International Space Station**

Narrator: Most people drive or take a bus, train, or subway to work.

But Sunita Williams is different.

Every morning she gets up, takes her dog for a walk, and gets ready for work. But sometimes when she goes to work, her vehicle is very unusual. Yes, it takes her 15–20 minutes with traffic to drive her car two miles to the office in Houston, Texas. But we're not talking about that vehicle or that office.

She has a special vehicle she takes to a different office, and traffic's not a problem. Captain Sunita Williams is an American astronaut. In 2012 she spent four months in a very special office—the International Space Station.

She traveled to the space station in this Russian Soyuz rocket.

The trip was 250 miles, straight up.

The trip to space took just nine minutes.

That's half the time it usually takes Sunita to drive to work.

Sunita Williams traveled in a tiny capsule on top of hundreds of tons of rocket power.

After she, Russian cosmonaut Yuri Malenchenko, and Japanese astronaut Akihiko Hoshide climbed the stairs and rode the elevator to the top, they went inside. Then it was time to blast off for the International Space Station.

Man: T-minus ten, nine, eight, seven, six, five, four, three, two, one.

Lift off. Lift off of the Soyuz TMA05M, carrying Suni Williams, Yuri Malenchenko, and Aki Hoshide on a journey to the International Space Station.

The authors and publishers acknowledge the following sources of copyright material and are grateful for the permissions granted. While every effort has been made, it has not always been possible to identify the sources of all the material used, or to trace all copyright holders. If any omissions are brought to our notice, we will be happy to include the appropriate acknowledgements on reprinting.

The publisher has used its best endeavors to ensure that the URLs for external websites referred to in this book are correct and active at the time of going to press. However, the publisher has no responsibility for the websites and can make no guarantee that a site will remain live or that the content is or will remain appropriate.

Photo Credits

The publishers are grateful to the following for permission to reproduce copyright photographs and material:

Key: T = Top, C = Center, B = Below, L = Left, R = Right, TL = Top Left, TR = Top Right, BL = Below Left, BR = Below Right, CL = Center Left, CR = Center Right

The following images are sourced from Getty Images.

pp. 14-15: Robert Loe/Moment; p. 16: Ak_Phuong/Moment; p. 17: Tetra Images; p. 18: Yongyuan Dai/Istock; p. 19 (TR): Xun Zhang/Contributor/Moment Mobile; p. 19 (CL): Dinodia Photo/Corbis Documentary; p. 19 (BR): Mohamed El-Shahed/Afp; p. 20: Jakkapan Prammanasik/Moment; pp. 22-23: Adam Jones/Photographer'S Choice; p. 22 (BR): Scott Olson; pp. 24-25: Marcduf/E+; p. 24: Frank Bienewald/Lightrocket; p. 25 (TL): Richard Theis/Eyeem; p. 25 (BR): Ramzi Haidar/Afp; p. 27: Greg Vaughn/Perspectives; pp. 28-29: Roberto Machado Noa/Lightrocket; p. 30: Seanpavonephoto/Istock; pp. 32-33: Himanshu Khagta/Moment; p. 32 (spot): Per-Andre Hoffmann/Look-Foto; p. 32 (spot): Rich-Joseph Facun/Arabianeye; p. 32 (spot): Robyn Breen Shinn/Cultura Exclusive; p. 32 (spot): Sollina Images/Blend Images; p. 34: Gpointstudio/Cultura; p. 35: Alan Copson/Photolibrary; p. 36 (TR): Mendowong Photography/Moment; p. 36 (CR): Sollina Images/The Image Bank; p. 36 (BR): Chia Hsien Lee/Eyeem; p. 37 (TR): Ariel Skelley/Photographer'S Choice; p. 37 (CR): Christopher Kimmel/Moment; p. 37 (BR): Andia/Universal Images Group; p. 39: Jeremy Woodhouse/Blend Images; pp. 40-41: Richard I'Anson/Lonely Planet Images; pp. 42-43 (BG): Gyro Photography/Amana Images; p. 42: Marwan Naamani/Afp; p. 43 (TL): John Elk/Lonely Planet Images; p. 45: Artur Widak/Nurphoto; p. 46: Liu Liqun/Corbis Documentary; p. 48: Garen Meguerian/Moment; pp. 50-51: Trevor Williams/Taxi Japan; p. 52: Alberto Buzzola/Lightrocket; p. 53: Tony Karumba/Afp; p. 54 (TL): Kelvin Murray/Taxi; p. 54 (TR): Andresr/E+; p. 54 (BR): Pbombaert/Moment; p. 55: Marco_Piunti/Istock; p. 56: Jetta Productions/Digitalvision; p. 58: Robtek/Istock Editorial; p. 59: Filadendron/E+; p. 60: Andersen Ross/Blend Images; p. 61 (CR): Klaus Vedfelt/Iconica; p. 61 (BR): Ian Lishman/Ian Lishman; p. 62: Jamie Grill/Jgi/Blend Images; p. 63: Justin Lewis/Stone; p. 65: Michael Short/Bloomberg; p. 66: Greg Lawler/Moment; pp. 68-69: Leonid_Tit/Istock; p. 68 (a): Bryan Mullennix/The Image Bank; p. 68 (b): Ariadne Van Zandbergen/Lonely Planet Images; p. 68 (c): BOISVIEUX Christophe/hemis.fr; p. 68 (d): Andre Gallant/Photographer'S Choice; pp. 70-71: Mitchell Krog/Gallo Images; p. 72 (T): John Finney Photography/Moment; p. 72 (CL): Planet Observer/Universal Images Group; p. 72 (BR): Cuellar/Moment; p. 73 (TL): Visual China Group; p. 73 (B): Andrew Mcconnell/Robertharding; p. 75: Planet Observer/Universal Images Group; pp. 76-77: Joe & Clair Carnegie/Libyan Soup/Moment; pp. 78-79: Westend61; p. 81: Skodonnell/E+; p. 84: John Finney Photography/Moment; p. 85: Niccolò

Ubalducci Photographer/Stormchaser/Moment; pp. 86-87: Paul Bradbury/Caiaimage; p. 88: Mark Bonifacio/Ny Daily News; p. 90: Peter Parks/Afp; p. 91: Andrew Pickett/Britain On View; p. 92: Cem Ozdel/Anadolu Agency; p. 93: Cem Oksuz/Anadolu Agency; pp. 94-95: Electra-K-Vasileiadou/Istock Editorial; p. 96 (T): Mike Hewitt; Sport; p. 96 (BR): Dan Mullan; p. 98: Jamie Mcdonald; p. 99: Marc Dozier/Corbis Documentary; p. 102: Seth K. Hughes/Image Source; pp. 104-105: Cecilie_Arcurs/E+; pp. 104 (spot): Chesnot News; pp. 104 (spot): David Ramos News; pp. 106-107: View Pictures/Uig; p. 109 (TL): Hero Images; p. 109 (TR): Yuri_Arcurs/Digitalvision; p. 109 (BL): Jetta Productions/Blend Images; p. 109 (BR): Alistair Berg/Digitalvision; p. 110: Peter Cade/The Image Bank; pp. 112-113: Reza Estakhrian/Iconica; p. 114: Justin Sullivan; News; p. 115 (BR): Kim Kulish/Corbis; p. 115 (TR): William Andrew/Photographer'S Choice; p. 119: Tim Robberts/The Image Bank; p. 120: Douglas Sacha/Moment; pp. 122-123: Hadynyah/E+; p. 122 (Spot): Sean Gallup News; p. 122 (Spot): Tim Graham/Tim Graham Photo Library; p. 122 (Spot): Ullstein Bild; p. 124: Matthew Staver/Bloomberg; p. 125: Carl Court; p. 126 (T): Westend61; p. 126 (CL): Justin Case/Taxi; p. 127 (TR): Fabrice Guerin/Biosphoto; p. 127 (BR): Sacramento Bee/Tribune News Service; p. 129 (BR): Luiz Rampelotto/Pacific Press/Lightrocket; p. 129 (CR): Andy Katz/Pacific Press/Lightrocke; p. 130: Steve Jennings; p. 131: Ernesto Mastrascusa/Latincontent; p. 132 (TL): Sean Gallup; News; p. 132 (BR): Stephen Pond; p. 132 (BG): Oxygen/Moment; p. 133 (BR): Sean Drakes/Con/Latincontent Editorial; p. 133 (TL): Christian Kober/Awl Images; p. 134: Christian Kober/Awl Images; pp. 136-137: Georgeclerk/E+; p. 138: John Greim/Lightrocket; p. 139: Robert Barnes/Moment Mobile; pp. 140-141: John Finney Photography/Moment; p. 142: Caspar Benson; p. 142 (Spot): Stan Honda/Afp Creative; p. 144 (BG): Natapong Supalertsophon/Moment; p. 144: Robyn Beck/Afp; p. 145 (BL): Bloomberg; p. 145 (TR): Mark Ralston/Afp; p. 146: Stocktrek Images; p. 147: Matjaz Slanic/E+; p. 148: Christophe Lehenaff/Photononstop; p. 150 (T): Detlev Van Ravenswaay/Picture Press; p. 150 (BL): Stocktrek Images; p. 151: Daniela Amaral/Eyeem; p. 154: Inigo Cia/Moment; p. 156: Nigel Killeen/Moment.

Illustrations

by Fiona Gowen p. 97 (map).

Video Supplied by BBC Worldwide Learning.

Video Stills Supplied by BBC Worldwide Learning.

Corpus

Development of this publication has made use of the Cambridge English Corpus (CEC). The CEC is a multi-billion word computer database of contemporary spoken and written English. It includes British English, American English, and other varieties of English. It also includes the Cambridge Learner Corpus, developed in collaboration with the University of Cambridge ESOL Examinations. Cambridge University Press has built up the CEC to provide evidence about language use that helps produce better language teaching materials.

Cambridge Dictionaries

Cambridge dictionaries are the world's most widely used dictionaries for learners of English. The dictionaries are available in print and online at dictionary.cambridge.org. Copyright © Cambridge University Press, reproduced with permission.

Typeset by QBS

Audio by John Marshall Media

INFORMED BY TEACHERS

Classroom teachers shaped everything about *Prism*. The topics. The exercises. The critical thinking skills. Everything. We are confident that *Prism* will help your students succeed in college because teachers just like you helped guide the creation of this series.

Prism Advisory Panel

The members of the *Prism* Advisory Panel provided inspiration, ideas, and feedback on many aspects of the series. *Prism* is stronger because of their contributions.

Gloria Munson
University of Texas, Arlington

Dinorah Sapp
University of Mississippi

Kim Oliver
Austin Community College

Christine Hagan
George Brown College/Seneca College

Wayne Gregory
Portland State University

Heidi Lieb
Bergen Community College

Julaine Rosner
Mission College

Stephanie Kasuboski
Cuyahoga Community College

GLOBAL INPUT

Teachers from more than 500 institutions all over the world provided valuable input through:

- Surveys
- Focus Groups
- Reviews